SABBAT
ENTERTAINING

SABBAT ENTERTAINING

Celebrating the Wiccan Holidays With Style

WILLOW POLSON

CITADEL PRESS
Kensington Publishing Corp.
www.kensingtonbooks.com

CITADEL PRESS books are published by

Kensington Publishing Corp.
850 Third Avenue
New York, NY 10022

All Kensington titles, imprints, and distributed lines are available at special quantity discounts for bulk purchases for sales promotions, premiums, fund-raising, educational, or institutional use. Special book excerpts or customized printings can also be created to fit specific needs. For details, write or phone the office of the Kensington special sales manager: Kensington Publishing Corp., 850 Third Avenue, New York, NY 10022, attn: Special Sales Department, phone 1-800-221-2647.

CITADEL PRESS is Reg. U.S. Pat. & TM Off.
The Citadel Logo is a trademark of Kensington Publishing Corp.

All photos and illustrations by the author.

First printing: September 2002
First paperback printing: June 2005

10 9 8 7 6 5 4 3 2 1

Printed in the United States of America

Library of Congress Control Number: 2002104312

ISBN 0-8065-2351-4

This book is dedicated to those who enjoy great friends,
great food, and great ritual. May you find joy and inspiration
in these pages!

Many Blessings on your Path

CONTENTS

PREFACE

The modern Witch is an average person who likes to entertain as much as anyone else. Many books have been written on various ways of entertaining for the annual spectrum of traditional Judeo-Christian holidays. Some are centered around holiday lore and some focus on food and recipes. And we as Witches and Wiccans can use some of the information in books we may find on Halloween parties or Easter celebrations, considering that many modern holidays stem from our own ancient ways. You may even uncover a book of non-Christian Yule activities or get a few ideas from an obscure volume on English customs or medieval festivals. The problem is that most entertaining and party books don't have any room for Pagan holidays that haven't become universally popular, such as Imbolc and Mabon. The authors of those books are most likely unaware that our eight sabbats even exist, let alone that anyone celebrates them and might wish for some ideas on how to celebrate them with others.

It is for the modern Witch that this book was created. Whether the event is an intimate ritual performed in the home by a tightly knit coven or a large public gathering in the local park, the activities, crafts, recipes, decorating ideas and information in each chapter will provide lots of ways to fill the festivities with holiday spirit.

Think about how much effort is spent every year on the Christmas/Yule season, ignoring the expensive trips to the mall or the toll that impulse shopping takes on your credit card. We lovingly bake mountains of cookies, wrap gifts until we run out of tape (I knew I should have bought the twelve-pack!), and spend days decorating house, office, yard, and ourselves. What if all this energy was divided among eight holidays instead of splurging everything on this one? As Witches we celebrate eight holidays, but most of us still fall into the old habit of having a simple ritual with minimal fanfare for the other seven, Samhain perhaps being the exception.

I love to play with garlands of silk flowers, cook just the right seasonal dish, string up festive mini lights and burn colorful candles any time of year! Yes, I still make a big deal out of Yule for my family with the tree and all that, but I also relish hanging my spring wreath on the door and decorating the kitchen with autumn-hued dried corn and oak leaves as the season demands. Why should we limit ourselves to what the card companies and variety stores dictate is an "official" holiday? Get creative and celebrate each of our own holidays with the energy and respect they deserve.

Throughout these pages, at the beginning of the sections for each sabbat, you will find diagrams for embroidering a square symbolizing that sabbat. These can be used simply as pillow covers or wall hangings, or they can be sewn together to make a Wheel of the Year quilt or wall hanging as illustrated in the *second* color insert (and see directions on page 215).

This book gives you the tools to add more to your sabbat celebrations. If you're hosting a public ritual, let the activities I've suggested become a part of the ceremony so that everyone can participate and experience the holiday more fully. If your home will be the site of a private sabbat for just you and a few covenmates, serve them the complete dinner menu from the appropriate chapter after the ritual. Sounds like too much work? It's probably less effort than you put into Yule each year, and I've designed most of the recipes to be easy to make with minimal fuss.

A word about these recipes—you may notice in thumbing through the book that all the recipes are meatless. I'm a vegetarian and didn't feel right providing recipes full of meat (and I couldn't exactly test them either). You are welcome to make any substitutions and additions you like however, such as using chicken broth instead of veg-etable broth or adding beef to the pot pies. Everything in this book is a jumping-off point and you should always feel free to play with the craft projects, activities, and recipes so that they please you most.

Change the materials, the size, the way it's done, the quantity, etc., to suit your needs, especially if you're working with a group. Make little embroidery kits out of the cross stitch patterns for people to take home, leave out the walnuts in a recipe if someone in your coven is allergic to them, use magnesium sticks instead of flint and steel if you're worried about the safety of the fire-starting contest, and double the honey lemonade recipe if you've got a thirsty crowd to cover.

While this book is meant to be a resource for the entire family, some projects require adult supervision and some should not be attempted by children at all. These projects call for supplies such as sharp knives, acid glass etching paste, hot wax, and wood gouges. Please use good judgment if you involve children in these crafts, and always use proper safety equipment when needed.

I hope this book enables you and those in your life to enjoy our sab-bats more fully and with added joy. So what are you waiting for? Let's get those busy hands working on some holiday fun!

ACKNOWLEDGMENTS

My sincere thanks go out to those that made this book possible— Craig, my wonderful husband who has always been behind me, beside me, and leading by example; Laney, the bestest grandma ever; Kathi, who watched my son with patience and grace so that I'd have time to work; my exceptional editor Margaret who was unfailingly kind, fought for what we both wanted, and always made me laugh; Angela at Reign Trading Co.; Aylene at the Running Thread; and many others who played a part in helping me get this book done, whether they know it or not. Of course, I'd also like to thank the deities who watch over me and give me nudges in the right direction, especially Lakshmi and Bast.

SABBAT
ENTERTAINING

1

YULE/WINTER SOLSTICE

(December 20–23)

For many people around the world, Yule or Christmas is the ultimate celebration, an extravagant orgy of food, gifts, celebration, and high spirits. What started out as a festival to honor the death and birth of the sun (and later the Son) also serves the purpose of helping people forget that it's the middle of winter and it will be many months before the spring planting can begin and fresh food is available.

While some hardy souls are out chopping firewood or tobogganing in frigid temperatures, or some are lamenting the loss of a tender plant forgotten outside in warmer climes, the Wheel of the Year spins on. The cycle of life and death, the spiral of time eternal, the needs of humans and nonhumans, ancestors and descendants . . . these all dance their way through the cold, dark universe on our little blue planet.

Perhaps more so than at harvest time we are drawn indoors to our homes and the homes of others. We nest and seek to curl up with something hot to eat or drink, burrowing inside the covers at night to hibernate with a loved one.

Then the moment draws near when the sun is so weak he can barely break through the clouds in the morning, and the longest night is close. Some will hold a vigil all night, singing and drumming, telling stories, serving special foods, and waiting for the sun to be reborn with the dawn. When the sun finally breaks the horizon on that auspicious morning, bells are rung in welcome and thanks, and people hold each other with joy at the beautiful sight, knowing that the Wheel has turned once again.

In Egyptian belief, the sun god Ra battles with the forces and demons of the underworld every night as he sails on his celestial boat. He survives by understanding and not fearing the darkness, and as the scarab Kephra transforms and is transformed by this nightly journey to become Ra once again in the morning, his boat eternally sailing across the skies like Apollo's chariot. A story about this transformative journey could be told during your own Yule night vigil along with other games and activities.

Of Trees and Traditions

Of course, the European Yule tree bedecked with jewels and lights is honoring both the returning light of the Sun King and the mystery of never-ending life, exemplified by the evergreen tree, whose leaves never turn yellow or fall away. The Yule log is another seasonal tradition, one that appears to have come down to us over the years from Scandinavia. There are many traditions related to the Yule log, varying slightly from region to region. But no one can deny that this simple piece of firewood has been held in esteem for centuries, and has only died out as an important Yule tradition with the decline of the open-hearth home fireplace and the gathering of firewood from the forest. We may gain efficient heating with stoves that burn gas between never-changing fake logs or little pellets of compressed sawdust, but we have lost the Yule log for the most part—except as a rolled cake dessert.

Finding and lighting the Yule log is a great activity for a family or group to do together, especially if one of you lives on or near land where a log can be gathered from the wild. Traditionally the Yule log must be found in the forest and never purchased, for that would bring bad luck. An oak log with holly kindling is the perfect (and very traditional) combination, for Yule is the time when the Oak King is born and takes over his reign from the winter Holly King.

With freshly washed hands, the new log is laid in the hearth atop the remnants of last year's Yule log (which has been carefully stored to protect the home from bad luck) and dry kindling. Use candle nubs, waxed pinecones, or other starters to help guarantee that the fire will start on the first attempt—if it doesn't, it foretells a year of ill fortune for the household. Once the Yule log is blazing merrily, sing songs to honor the Old Gods and the newborn sun. One tradition is to toss sprigs of holly into the fire with wishes for a safe, lucky, and trouble-free new year.

The Yule log and fire is the perfect centerpiece for your solstice festivities. In some places the fire is traditionally burned and tended for twelve hours, perfect for an all-night vigil. There are many activities that can be connected to the Yule log, from gathering the wood, to starting the fire, to simply watching the shadows created by the flames. And don't forget to save some of this year's log for next year!

Hand Shadows

Think for a moment how ancient it must be for people to make shadow shapes on the walls with their hands. Did the Neanderthals make shadow plays of the quick antelope or the ponderous mammoth, moving their fingers skillfully to give the impression of life?

Hand shadows are an age-old children's pastime, but skillful adults have also enjoyed crafting difficult shapes, especially in Victorian times when simple family entertainments were in vogue. Books are available (see Resources) for how to make both simple shadows that children can master up to difficult animals and objects that even dexterous grown-ups will need to practice at. This is a great way to entertain your guests (and they can entertain each other) during an all-night solstice vigil.

Silhouette Puppets

In some countries, such as Indonesia and Bali, traditional folk tales and legends are told using two-dimensional puppets on sticks. A translucent screen is lit from behind, and the puppets are held against the screen as they're moved to tell the story. The audience sees the entire performance as black silhouette puppets, the proximity to the screen cleverly used to show distance, depth, and size changes. A modern version you and your children may have seen is on the Disney television show "Bear in the Big Blue House," when Bear's friend Shadow (a projected silhouette herself) tells a story in song using jointed silhouette puppets.

Make some puppets of your own and tell a sacred legend with them. Have two or three of your party help work the puppets, make sound effects, narrate, or otherwise help run the show. For added effect, you can set the stage in front of the fireplace or some tiki torches for a golden, flickering light.

Flint-and-Steel Firestarting Contest

As messy as it is, starting a fire by hand with flint and steel is a great way to reenact those tense moments long ago when the tribe's fire was ritually extinguished each solstice night and then relit with skill and a sigh of relief. It also makes terrific ritual theater if your group has an outdoor bonfire on Yule.

This activity must be done outside so you don't end up with sharp bits of flint all over the floor. You'll also need eye protection in case a flint flake or bit of steel flips upward accidentally.

The easiest way to get a flint-and-steel fire started is by using char-cloth, which you can make yourself with things you may already have around the house. Find some 100 percent cotton cloth, such as old diapers, thin "Warm & Natural" quilt batting, T-shirts, etc. (I used my husband's old underwear and it worked great). Be sure it's not treated with flame retardant chemicals or it won't burn as desired—test it by setting a match to a corner of the fabric and see if it's eager to start or if it seems sluggish.

Cut the cotton into four-inch squares and set aside. Find an old pan, preferably cast iron, with a tight-fitting lid. Using tongs to hold the fabric at one corner, light the bottom edges and allow it to burn just until flame spreads evenly across the surface and it begins to blacken. Place the fabric into the pan and place the lid on tightly. Let set for about 30 seconds to allow the flame to use all the oxygen inside the pan. Open the lid carefully, closing it again immediately if there are any flames left. You're trying to create a square of cloth with few or no uncharred areas that will burn easily. Charcloth is a bit fragile to store, so try keeping the cloths stacked in a rigid lidded container until you're ready to use them.

This is just like lighting any candles you want to use in a public ritual in advance so that they will catch quickly and easily when the time comes. The charcloth catches the tiny spark made when you hit the flint and steel together and will help the fire start more easily. It's still very tricky to get a real flame by using flint and steel, so this contest is great fun among all ages.

Each participant will need a stone circle or other hearth to burn their fire inside, eye protection, a flint and steel set (available online or at many historic sites and reenactment merchants), at least one piece of charcloth (make extra in case nobody can do it at first), bits of finely shredded tissue paper or other fuzzy burnable material, small twigs or pine needles, and a few pencil-size twigs.

Make sure you've practiced this yourself so you can show everyone how it's done. Set people several feet apart and have them first lay down a piece of charcloth where they will be starting their fire. Lay out their materials in order of size within reach. Have them grip the steel in one hand, the flint in the other, and give the signal to begin.

Technique is everything! The idea is to shave off a tiny bit of steel with the sharp flint stone, so you don't want to just knock the things together caveman style—hit the steel with the very edge of the flint, using long strokes and aiming toward the charcloth. An alternate method is to hold the flint edge side up and hit the steel against it in a sweeping motion; which way you do it is purely a matter of personal preference.

Ideally the steel spark should hit the charcloth and begin to burn for a moment. Once a spark makes it onto the charcloth, the participants will need to blow on the spark very gently to help it grow inside the cloth, then feed it with the fuzzy bits of tissue or whatever you have provided for this first stage of kindling (see photo in the first color insert). As the smoke (hopefully) grows, they should keep blowing gently on the smoke and put in a few tiny twigs or pine needles. The first one to get a real orange flame wins the contest and gets to light the bonfire.

Orange Passing Game

Oranges, when available, have long been treasured as part of Yule festivities. A popular party game is "Passing the Orange," and as Witches we can enjoy not only the fun of the game, we can look more deeply for the symbolism within. The orange represents the golden orb of the Sun King, so sweet in his summer gifts to us and so longed for in winter. As we pass the orange from person to person, see it as the passing of the old year to the new, on and on through the seasons and the years.

Have your guests stand in rows of all the same number (if you have fifteen guests, have them stand in three rows of five, and so on). Give the first person in each row an orange to hold under his or her chin without using hands to help. The object of the game is to pass the orange to the chin of next person in the row without using hands, and so on, until the last person has the orange under his or her chin and successfully drops it in a container at the end of the row. The first row to finish gets a prize.

Mistletoe

The use of mistletoe as a sacred plant began with the Druids, who still carefully gather the plant with special sickles and catch it as it falls so that it doesn't touch the ground. So where did the tradition of kissing under the mistletoe begin?

Mistletoe is a medicinal herb, thought to bestow good health and fertility, and it is also used as a ward against poison and evil spirits. The first time we see the tradition of kissing under the plant to gain fertility and good luck is in the Roman festival of Saturnalia, which was later replaced by Christmas as Rome converted to Christianity. The Victorians, who propagated many of our modern Yuletide traditions, liked to re-create ancient traditions (especially from ancient Greece and Rome) and popularized the idea of kissing under the mistletoe late in the nineteenth century, sometimes citing the Greek tradition that it signifies a promise to marry.

There is also a legend from Scandinavia, where mistletoe is considered the plant of peace and truce, that may be another explanation as to why we kiss under the mistletoe. Freya (or Frigga, depending on the version of the story) made sure that everything from the land and air and water could not hurt her son Balder. But the mistletoe, which is a parasite of trees and grows in none of those places, was overlooked, and an arrow was made from mistletoe. Balder was shot and killed by the arrow, but Freya brought him back to life. She was so happy that she proclaimed that everyone passing under the mistletoe must receive a kiss and that no harm would come to them.

Besides kissing under it, give your guests a sprig to take home with them for good luck, fertility, and to ward off evil. Try to find a version of the Freya legend that would be good for storytelling or even make a mystery play out of it.

Twelfth Night and Wassailing

Not celebrated much in the United States except by Catholics and living-history buffs, Twelfth Night is still remembered in Britain and Europe, although we across the pond do still sing "The Twelve Days of Christmas." Twelfth Night is probably an offshoot of the Roman Saturnalia. This wild party, which took place proceeding the solstice, lasted for a week and was filled with wine, women, and song. The Christians celebrate the twelfth day after Christmas day as Epiphany and the day that the three wise men visited Jesus and gave their gifts. In New Orleans, carnival season begins on Twelfth Night with parades, the electing of a Rex (King of Carnival) and Queen, and the baking of King Cakes. These cakes may have originally been baked to honor the Sun King, the three wise men (who were also kings), or Jesus as Christ the King.

A popular Yuletide activity, often carried out until Twelfth Night, is wassailing. A wassail is a large bowl of mixed beverages, and I've heard that this is either a specially concocted alcoholic punch of ale and other ingredients, or is a mélange of whatever the wassailers ended up with in their bowl after going door to door and getting donations poured in. The latter sounds rather revolting to me, but I guess when you've been walking all over town on a freezing night drinking and singing, you're ready for anything. Wassailing is the origin of today's door-to-door caroling, although the modern version is often more like trick-or-treating, with children asking for coins or candy rather than alcohol.

There are several well-known wassail songs, although most of us are more familiar with the melody than the words. Here are the words to a common one many people know, simply titled "The Wassail Song" (you can change the deity gender if you like):

Here we come a-wassailing among the leaves so green,
Here we come a-wandering so fair to be seen.

(Chorus)

Love and joy come to you,
And to your wassail too,
And God bless you and send you a happy new year,
And God send you a happy new year.

We are not daily beggars who beg from door to door,
But we are neighbor's children whom you have seen before.

(Chorus)

We have a little purse made of ratching leather skin,
We want some of your small change to line it well within.

(Chorus)

God bless the master of this house, likewise the mistress too,
And all the little children that round the table go.

(Chorus)

Another wassail song, whose tune is found on the first Mannheim Steamroller Christmas album (1984) as the first verse of "Wassail, Wassail," is the "Gloucestershire Wassail":

Wassail, wassail, all over the town,
Our bread it is white and our ale it is brown;
Our bowl it is made of the good maple tree,
From the wassailing bowl we'll drink unto thee.

Come, butler, and fill us a bowl of your best,
And we hope your soul in Heaven may rest;
But if you do bring us a bowl of the small,
Then down shall go butler and bowl and all.

Come here, sweet maid, in the frilly white smock,
Come trip to the door and trip back the lock!
Come trip to the door and pull back the pin,
And let us jolly wassailers in.

One Twelfth Night wassailing tradition still practiced in parts of England is the wassailing of the apple trees, first recorded in 1585, when it had already long been a part of popular culture. The traditional date for wassailing of the apple trees is January 17 (Twelfth Night by the old calendar); you might perform it on Yule, Twelfth Night, or Imbolc. Last year's apple cider is carried out to the apple orchard in a large bucket, along with bread, cups for dipping, and a shotgun or a handful of stones. The bread is dipped in the cider and hung in the branches of the tree for the red-breasted robins, who represent the apple tree spirits. The tree is then toasted and splashed with the cider to bless the tree and ensure a good, healthy harvest. Like so many ancient traditions, the spirits are given both a carrot and a stick—besides giving gifts and blessing the tree, handfuls of rocks are hurled or a shotgun blast is aimed up into the tree to discourage any ill spirits and make them think twice about harming the apples. A chant is then sung around the tree. If you can't find a traditional one, use one of the two above or make up your own. The rest of the cider is then shared and the participants drink to each other's health and that of the orchard. Wassail!

CRAFTS

Yule Cross Stitch

The Oak King and Holly King cross paths at midwinter, when the sky is blackest and change is in the air. Thirteen separate floss colors create a rich tapestry to reflect the season's hidden wealth. (For additional stitchery instructions, see pages 211–214.)

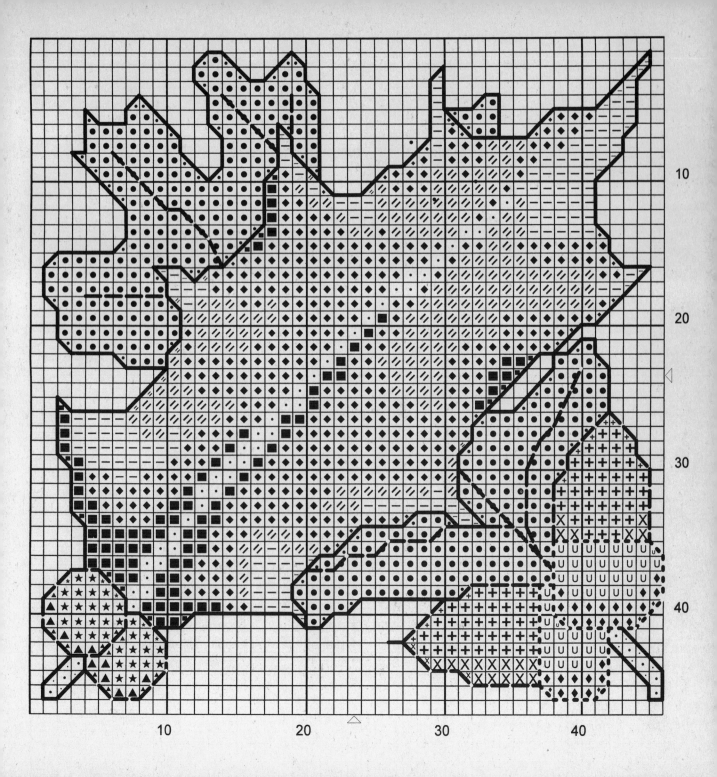

Grid Size: 47 W × 47 H
Cloth Count: 18
Fabric: Black Aida
Design Area: 2.61″ W × 2.61″ H (45 × 45 stitches)

Pattern Key

Symbol	DMC Floss		Color
■	986	(2 strands)	Forest green—very dark
◆	987	(2 strands)	Forest green—dark
∥	368	(2 strands)	Pistachio green—light
−	966	(2 strands)	Baby green—medium
·	704	(2 strands)	Chartreuse—bright
★	666	(2 strands)	Christmas red—bright
▲	498	(2 strands)	Christmas red—dark
+	435	(2 strands)	Brown—very light
X	433	(2 strands)	Brown—medium
U	612	(2 strands)	Drab brown—light
◆	610	(2 strands)	Drab brown—dark
•	989	(2 strands)	Forest green

Backstitches

Backstitch around the shapes as noted below.

Shape	DMC Floss		Color
Leaf outline	986	(1 strand)	Forest green—very dark
Oak leaf vein	987	(1 strand)	Forest green—dark
Acorns	433	(1 strand)	Brown—medium
Acorn caps	610	(1 strand)	Drab brown—dark
Holly berries	814	(1 strand)	Garnet—dark

Tissue Paper Robins

A traditional English decoration for Yule, often made by children, is the tissue paper robin, symbolizing a messenger and herald of spring, as well as functioning as an apple tree spirit. These are made in much the same way as the "stained glass windows" constructed in many grade schools and consist of torn bits of colored tissue that are glued together to make the robin. The resulting image is then hung in the window, where the light will make the image glow merrily.

YOU'LL NEED:

Tissue paper in brown, red or scarlet, light tan or light gray,
    yellow and green
Vellum or thin typing paper
White glue or glue stick
Scissors
Black construction paper

You can either tear the tissue paper into tiny random bits or tear it into the shapes you want. Look at a picture of a real robin and try to imitate the color arrangement—yellow for the beak, brown for the upper body and tail, red for the breast, tan for the underside of the body, and green grass or an evergreen for scenery. Glue the tissue paper bits to the vellum to make the picture. Make a frame for the picture out of the construction paper by cutting out the center to fit the image (smaller than the edges of the vellum), then glue the frame to the edges of the picture. Have everyone make one to take home and enjoy.

Paper Cornucopias

This simple craft was very popular in Victorian times, and the resulting ornaments were hung in the Yuletide tree (a new fad at the time) and filled with candy or small prizes, much like stockings are used today. You can leave the tops open and fill with flowers or other decorations, or fill the cornucopias with surprises and fold the tops over attractively for later enjoyment. In the first photo insert there's a picture of two I made. Use ribbons for hanging them or simply balance the cornucopias among the branch tips.

YOU'LL NEED:

Decorative papers, gift wrap, lace doilies, recycled art projects, etc.
Length of string
Pen or pencil
Scissors
Paper edger scissors (optional)
Tape
Lace, trims, stickers, etc. (optional)
Tacky craft glue (optional)
Ribbon (optional)

Cut a square of paper any size you like—the width of the paper is the finished height of the cornucopia. Wrap or tie the string around the pen, and place the pen's tip at one corner of the square. Use your finger to hold the string down at an adjacent corner and draw an arc to the corner opposite from where your pen starts drawing. You will have a quarter-circle pie slice shape. Using regular or edger scissors, cut along this line.

Form a cone shape (the curved edge is the top/open edge of the cone) and use a small piece of tape on the inside of the seam to secure it near the top edge. Pull down on the point of the cone if necessary to coax the paper into a perfect cone shape. Place another small piece of tape on the outside of the bottom tip, wrapping it around the point to provide added strength and protect against crushing and wear. Lay the cone on a table and place one last piece of tape on the inside of the seam halfway between the top and bottom. Now you can glue some lace trim to the top edge if you like (remember that it's a curved edge, so you may need to run some basting stitches and gather the edge of the lace to fit properly), leave it plain, or fill the cornucopia with goodies and fold over the top in quarters, using a decorative holiday sticker or bow to seal it.

Silhouette Puppets and Stage

This is a simple project that you can complete in advance, or you can have each guest make his own. You can all agree on a story or theme in advance, or just have each puppet get behind the screen one at a time and improvise.

YOU'LL NEED:

Cardstock paper, cereal boxes, posterboard, etc.
Scissors, both standard 8-inch desk ones and small pointed ones
Paper punches (standard round and optional decorative punches)
Small paper fasteners
Feathers, fake fur, fringe, etc., for decorating
Glue gun
1 36-inch-long ¼-inch-diameter dowel for each puppet
Very large cardboard box
Large piece of white paper, like butcher paper
Masking tape
Bright lamp, brightly blazing fireplace, or several lamps, candles, etc.

For each puppet, cut out a head/body piece, two upper arms, and two lower arms with hands (simple puppets without joints, such as trees, clouds, objects, etc. can also be made). Make the ends of the joints rounded so they don't catch on each other when the arms are moved. Punch holes in the body for facial features, jewelry, etc. and trim them to shape with the smaller scissors. Punch holes at the shoulders and elbows, then connect the five pieces to make the body and jointed arms. Glue on any decorations you like, always remembering that the puppets will be seen in silhouette for the show. Cut the dowel into one 6-inch piece and two 15-inch pieces, then securely glue the short piece to the bottom of the body and the two longer pieces to the backs of the hands. Allow to cool and set while you make the stage.

Cut the flaps off your box, then decide which side will be the top. Set the box so that the open end faces where the actors will sit. Cut a square hole in the upper edge of the bottom of the box so that you can sit comfortably on the floor behind the cardboard and not block the hole above you—place the box up on a coffee table if necessary to get the height you need. Using glue or masking tape, cover the hole you cut with the white paper, making sure to get it nice and flat in the opening.

To perform your play, set the lamp behind the stage (where the actors are) or place the stage in front of a bright fireplace. Hold your puppet in one hand by the shorter dowel, and hold both arm dowels in your other hand. Operate the arms together and practice a bit if you like before doing your play. Besides people with arms and static objects, try making monsters with hinged jaws, horses with jointed legs, birds with moving wings, and so on. Let your imagination fly free!

Yule Log Candleholders

These simple, rustic tealight holders can also be drilled to fit votive cups and even small pillar candles. They make a lovely Yule log if you don't have a fireplace to burn the real thing, and of course they also make great gifts.

YOU'LL NEED:

Attractive natural log, such as a small (3-inch diameter) oak
    or birch log with bark on
Hand saw or electric band saw
Hole saw to fit candle (1$\frac{1}{2}$-inch fits a tealight)
Electric drill or drill press
$\frac{1}{4}$-inch wood chisel and mallet
Spray varnish
Greenery, glitter, and other decorations
Glue gun (for decorations, optional)
Candles or glass votive cups to fit

You can either position these holders on end and cut them shorter or lay them down and make multiple candle holes in the side. After you decide on which position you want, saw the log to 3 inches long for an "on end" arrangement or to 12 inches for a long arrangement. Make very sure the log will not wobble or tip when finished—cut away where needed on the bottom to ensure a steady, safe candleholder.

For the standing log, drill one hole 1 inch deep into the end of the log (use a piece of tape on the hole saw to mark this exactly). For the horizontal log, drill three 1-inch deep holes along the length of the log. Carefully chisel out the cut circle and smooth the bottom of the hole. Evenly coat the candleholder with spray varnish (try to find water-based or, better yet, natural and environmentally friendly varnish). Decorate the log as desired. Place the log where you want it displayed, place the candles or holders within the holes and lay greenery around it, making sure it will not be near the burning candles.

Reuseable Gift Sacks

Remember that mountain of gift wrap you had to get rid of last year? How much of it was made from recycled paper? How much of it did you recycle? How much was simply used once and then ended up at the landfill? Make some festive fabric sacks to wrap your gifts in and help take some of the strain off Mother Earth too. It's so easy you'll find yourself making lots of these bags in different fabrics and sizes. All seam allowances are $1/4$ inch.

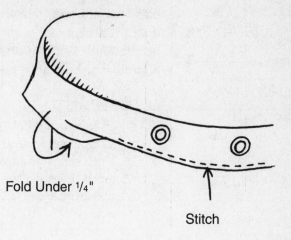

Fold Under $1/4$"

Stitch

YOU'LL NEED:

$1/4$ yard fabric (or more for a taller sack)
Scissors
Matching thread
Iron and ironing board
Eyelet setter (optional)
8 or 12 eyelets (optional)
$1/2$ yard ribbon

Wash and dry the fabric. Cut a circle 8 inches in diameter and one long rectangle 9 × 24 inches. Fold the rectangle in half, right sides of the fabric together, making a rectangle 9 × 12 inches. Stitch the ends together (short 9-inch sides) to form a large tube, then press the seam open and flat. Fold under the top edge (one of the long sides) of the tube ½ inch, then fold under again 1½ inches. Stitch this edge down about ¼ inch from the edge of the first fold and press flat. Stitch the unfolded edge of the tube to the circle, right sides together, and press the seam allowance away from the bottom when done. Turn the bag right side out.

Spacing them evenly, set the eyelets or make small buttonholes along the top edge where the fabric is doubled. Weave the ribbon in and out of the eyelets, then tie the ends of the ribbon in a square knot to make a large loop. To use, place your present inside (padding with tissue paper if desired) draw up the ribbons, and tie both ribbons in a single overhand knot or slip knot.

Kissing Ball

Many kissing balls are made of boxwood and pine to be decorative, or balsam and fruits to be fragrant. This variation uses mistletoe as well as fragrant accents for a lovely and unforgettable addition to your holiday decorations. You can also use greenery from your yard to personalize your kissing ball (see photo in first insert).

YOU'LL NEED:

5-inch square block of Oasis floral foam
Heavy wrapped floral wire
25 3-inch sprigs mistletoe
15 3-inch sprigs assorted fragrant greens (bay laurel,
    balsam, incense cedar, etc.)
Ice pick

6 fresh tangerines
Whole cloves
Thin floral wire
Floral picks
21 cranberries
$\frac{1}{2}$ yard 1-inch wide ribbon and straight pins (optional)

Cut the corners off the foam block so that it's roughly rounded, then soak it in water until saturated. Wrap the heavy floral wire around the foam like you would a package, so that four strands of wire make a cage around the foam. Make a sturdy loop at the top for hanging the finished ball.

Cut the ends of the sprigs at an angle so that they will penetrate the foam more easily and soak up more water, which will help them stay fresh longer. Evenly distribute the mistletoe springs all over the foam ball, pushing them into place securely. Fill in any bare spots with sprigs of the other greens, spacing them evenly around the ball.

Using the ice pick, pierce the tangerines in decorative or random patterns on one side of the fruit, then insert a whole clove into each hole, studding the tangerine. Use the ice pick to make a hole all the way through the center of the tangerine, then thread a length of the thin wire through the hole. Twist this wire into a loop so that the tangerine is like a bead on a string, then twist the cut ends of the wire onto a floral pick securely. Push the pick deeply into the foam, turning the fruit so that the clove-studded side faces outward.

Pierce the cranberries with the wire and twist to make a loop, attach to floral picks and use to fill in any remaining bare spots. If desired, add lengths of ribbon by either looping them over the greenery or letting them hang free and cutting the ends in an inverted **V** shape. If you hang your kissing ball in a cool location (not over a heater vent!) and water it occasionally, it will last for a few weeks.

Paper Animals

I taught myself how to make these whimsical confections after attending a music conference in Berkeley. One of the entertainers at the dinner was going around to all the tables and asking people what their favorite animal was. She would then cut the animals out of origami paper, fold them, and presto! They make great playthings for the little ones and colorful decorations too. A few are pictured in the first photo insert.

YOU'LL NEED:

1 package assorted origami or other one-sided colored papers
Carbon paper (optional)
Small sharp scissors, like embroidery scissors
Miniature specialty paper punch such as heart, star, diamond, etc.
  (optional)
Assorted fine-tip markers (optional)

Until you can cut the designs out on your own, trace an animal pattern onto a piece of origami paper with the carbon paper. Cut out the animal pattern shape, turning and pivoting the paper, not the scissors. Add punched accents and draw on features if desired.

Fold the papers on the center crease to add dimension to the animal, folding things like ears and manes backwards to the white side, then folding the adjacent parts like heads back to the colored side. Fold so that the paper ends up in the direction you are looking for—if you don't want that horse's tail to stick straight up, don't let it! Fold it backwards while flat and gently press the sides of the fold flat while you hold the body part where you want it. Adjust the angles of some parts, then do all flat folds last, such as ears and wings. For curved tails, run the paper across the edge of your fingernail on the inside of the curve.

Once you get the hang of it, try making different animals than the patterns given here. It just takes a little forethought and creativity.

Pegasus

Horse

Mouse

Cat

Dog

MENU

Winter Vegetable "Stoup"

Whole-Wheat Buns

Memories of Summer Fruit Salad

Persimmon Cranberry Quick Bread

Pomegranate Pie

Golden Sun Cookies

Spiked Hot Cocoa

Assorted Hot Teas

Winter Vegetable "Stoup"

My dad used to say "stoup" is any dish "too thick for soup, and too thin for stew." I've combined several veggies that are available in winter, either in your garden or in the stores, to make a delicious hearty "stoup" to warm the heart and the stomach. You are free, naturally, to use any winter vegetables you like best in this recipe.

1 tablespoon vegetable oil	1 large parsnip, cut into fat slices
1 small yellow onion, chopped	1 large stalk colored chard, chopped
2 cloves garlic, minced	
1 15-ounce can vegetable broth	1/4 cup rice
2 carrots, cut into chunks	
2 large or 3 small red potatoes, skin on, cut into chunks	

Heat the oil in a large saucepot over medium-high heat, then add onions. Sauté until just transparent, then add garlic. Cook 1 more minute or until garlic just begins to brown slightly. Add the broth and remaining ingredients. Bring to a boil, then turn down to low, and simmer for about 30 minutes or until all vegetables are tender. Serve hot with fresh whole wheat bread or rolls. 4 servings.

Whole-Wheat Buns

These UFO-shaped rolls are perfect for dipping in soups or tearing apart with your hands, medieval style.

1	tablespoon yeast	1	teaspoon salt
1½	cups hot water	¼	cup honey
About 4 cups whole-wheat flour		2	tablespoons melted butter

In a small bowl, combine the yeast and water, set aside. In a large bowl, combine the flour and salt. When the yeast has softened, pour the yeast, water, honey, and melted butter into the flour and mix thoroughly with a wooden spoon until well combined and the dough pulls away from the sides of the bowl. Turn out onto a well-floured surface and knead for 5–10 minutes. Cut the dough into 2-inch pieces and form each one into a 3–4-inch-wide flat circle. Place these circles on nonstick cookie sheets and allow to rise for about 30 minutes. Bake the buns, turning the sheets around halfway through baking as needed, at 375 degrees F. for about 20 minutes or until a nice medium-brown crust has formed and the buns sound hollow when tapped. Makes about 15–20 buns.

Memories of Summer Fruit Salad

Indulge in something unexpected in the middle of winter—a summery fruit salad. This combination of sunny fruits will remind you of the Sun King's climax as you celebrate his birth.

2 kiwi fruit, peeled, halved lengthwise, and sliced thick
1 banana, skin removed and sliced thick
1 navel orange, peeled and cut into bite-size chunks
1 cup fresh pineapple chunks
1 cup green seedless grapes
1 cup red seedless grapes
1 medium apple, peeled and cut into bite-size chunks

1/3 cup golden raisins
1/4 cup blueberries (or any other kind of small berry)
1/4 cup light mayonnaise
1/4 cup walnuts, chopped
2 tablespoons mixed dried fruit bits
Mint sprigs for garnish (optional)

Combine all ingredients except the nuts and dried fruit bits in a large bowl and gently toss to evenly distribute the mayonnaise. Transfer the salad to a serving bowl and sprinkle the nuts and dried fruit bits on top. The raisins will soften and plump a bit if the salad is stored in the refrigerator for about 15–30 minutes. Garnish with fresh mint if desired. 4 to 6 servings.

Persimmon Cranberry Quick Bread

If you think this combination of tart fruits will overwhelm, never fear— Hachiya persimmons are sensationally sweet when fully ripe and offset the tangy cranberries perfectly. This loaf also makes a wonderful holiday gift.

2½	cups flour	2	eggs
1½	cups sugar	¼	cup butter, melted
2	teaspoons baking powder	¼	cup milk
½	teaspoon baking soda	1	cup chopped cranberries
½	teaspoon salt	½	cup chopped pecans
2	Hachiya persimmons, very soft ripe (like an overripe tomato)		(optional)

Preheat oven to 350 degrees F. Grease and flour a medium loaf pan or place greased cupcake papers in muffin tins. Combine all dry ingredients in a medium bowl. Cut the persimmons in half and scrape the soft pulp out of the halves with a spoon, placing the skins cut side up on a cutting board so you can scrape the last bits of pulp off them to finish. Purée the pulp in a food processor until smooth and liquid. Pour the pulp into a large bowl, then add the eggs, butter, and milk. Stir in dry ingredients until moistened. Add the cranberries and nuts, then spread the batter in the loaf pan or drop by spoonfuls into papered muffin tins. Bake the loaf for at least one hour or until the center tests done. Cool at least 10 minutes before removing from the pan and serving. Bake muffins for 20–25 minutes or until they test done. Makes one medium loaf or about 16 muffins.

Pomegranate Pie

Your guests will be asking for seconds (and the recipe) when you serve them a slice of this delicious pink parfait pie. The flavor is delightfully delicate and it's a festive favorite for the whole family—my finicky four-year-old son loves it.

Prebaked plain or graham pie crust

FOR THE FILLING

- 1 egg
- 1 14-ounce can sweetened condensed milk
- 2 tablespoons agar powder or unflavored gelatin
- 1 cup sugar
- 1 cup fresh pomegranate juice (from about 2 large pomegranates)
- 1 tablespoon lemon juice
- 1 teaspoon grenadine syrup or raspberry-flavored syrup
- 1 cup whipping cream

Whipped cream and pomegranate seeds for garnish

Place the precooked pie shell in the refrigerator to chill. Soak the agar powder in one tablespoon of warm water to soften. To juice the pomegranates, cut them in half and place them face down in a large bowl, then press down on them firmly with two hands to crush the juice out of them. Pomegranate juice stains like grape juice, so wear an apron. Use a wire mesh strainer over your liquid measuring cup to strain out the seed pulp.

In a medium saucepan, whisk together the egg and milk until blended. Add the agar and sugar, then cook over medium-high until the agar and sugar dissolve completely and the mixture is quite hot (but not boiling). Reduce heat to low and continue cooking, stirring constantly, for about 5 minutes or until it begins to thicken a bit and occasional bubbles form on the surface. Do not let the mixture scorch on the bottom or you'll find brown bits in your pie. Remove from heat and pour into a medium bowl. Stir in the pomegranate juice, lemon juice, and syrup. Chill until the mixture begins to gel, about 2 hours.

Whip the cream to soft peaks, then fold it gently and completely into the pomegranate mixture. Spoon gently into the chilled pie crust and chill for several hours or until completely set. Serve with a dollop of whipped cream and a sprinkling of pomegranate seeds. Store in the refrigerator. 6–8 servings.

Golden Sun Cookies

If you can't find a sun-shaped cookie cutter, just use a round one and pipe faces and rays out of yellow icing onto the circles. Or if your artistry with an icing bag isn't something you want to show your guests, frost the cookies all orange and declare them "The Solar Disk of Ra."

2½ cups flour	¼ cup shortening
1 teaspoon baking powder	1 egg
½ teaspoon baking soda	1 teaspoon vanilla
¼ teaspoon salt	½ teaspoon lemon extract
¼ teaspoon cinnamon	¼ teaspoon orange extract
1 cup sugar	1 tablespoon finely grated lemon peel
½ cup fat-free sour cream	
¼ cup butter, softened	

In a medium bowl, combine the flour, baking powder, soda, salt, and cinnamon until blended. In a large bowl, mix together the remaining ingredients, then stir in the flour mixture, kneading it a few times if necessary to completely combine the ingredients. Roll out the dough on a floured surface and cut into sun or circle shapes. Use nonstick cookie sheets or very lightly mist regular sheets with nonstick cooking spray. Place the cookies on the sheets and bake at 425 degrees F. for 6–8 minutes or until the edges just start to turn golden. Remove the cookies from the baking sheets and cool completely on wire racks, then frost as desired. Makes about 3 dozen cookies.

Spiked Hot Cocoa

Why have boring hot cocoa? Dress up any recipe for this perfect winter beverage by adding a few of your favorite things (and I don't mean whiskers on kittens or brown paper packages tied up with string). My absolute ultimate hot cocoa mix is Ghirardelli's Double Chocolate—I think it's even better than homemade recipes without the hassle and mess; of course you can use any cocoa recipe you prefer.

Things I have added to hot chocolate with great success are: marshmallow crème (the kind in the jar); a sprinkle of cinnamon (a.k.a. Mexican cocoa); freshly grated nutmeg; flavored syrups like vanilla, raspberry, or hazelnut; malted milk powder; orange (or almond or rum or any other flavor) extract; and others I'm sure I'm forgetting.

Don't use all these at the same time! Experiment and see what tickles your fancy, perhaps starting off with one at a time and then combining two, like cinnamon with orange syrup, or marshmallow crème with a dusting of chocolate powder on top. What interesting additions can you think of that I haven't listed here?

DECORATIONS

Honeycomb paper suns: You've seen them in the supermarkets, now haunt your local party supply place in the summer to start collecting these perfect solstice decorations. But don't pack them too far away when winter's over—they're perfect for summer solstice too.

Sun patio lights: These may be tricky to find, but even one string of these hung in the window or over your buffet table will delight your guests. They are really just strings of mini lights with plastic sun-shaped covers. Of course, any kind of holiday lights look great all over the house. I especially enjoy using the vintage Lighted Ice, Snowballs, frosted pastel C-7s, and bubble lights that were my grandfather's to decorate my home for Yule.

Winter fruits: Fresh or fake, winter fruits like persimmons, apples, pears, pomegranates, lady apples, and various nuts look terrific on the table or on the tree. I especially like the glittery ones that look like they're sugared or the opulent beaded ones. They make me want to just pick them up and eat them!

Dried fruits: Apple rings strung like beads make a wonderful garland, especially when combined with whole cinnamon sticks. Other dried fruits, like orange slices and raisins, also make beautiful garlands and are perfect for hanging on trees outside so the birds can enjoy the solstice too.

Fresh cut greens: Shh! Don't tell anyone, but I've been known to creep up on unsuspecting Christmas tree lots and sneak off with armloads of discarded evergreen branches! I also love going out into the woods and collecting wild greens, such as bay laurel, toyon (also called Christmas berry), live oak, and various pine boughs. What winter greens are native to your area? Clip a few branches of each and bring them inside, or place a huge armload into a decorated bucket full of water for your front porch. The possibilities are endless for fresh cut greens!

Garlands: I love the look of luxurious garlands over doorways, windows, mantles and even draping over the table. Intertwine fresh greens with wired strings of golden stars, twist several strings of wooden or glass beads together for a swag, or use whimsical strands of candy or fruit around the house in surprising places.

Candles: What would Yule be without candles? Use them everywhere (with caution, of course—it ruins the holiday spirit to have the house burn down). If your fireplace is out of commission, fill the empty hearth with candles! Use floating candles in water-filled bowls in the bathroom, regal tapers on the buffet table, fat multi-wicked pillars on end tables, and luminaria bags all along your front walk.

Pinecones: There are few things in nature more structured and interesting to look at than the humble pinecone. A true symbol of the season, pinecones begin to drop in late fall or early winter and come in hundreds of shapes and sizes. Pile them in a basket by the fireplace (if you have loads, they make great fire starters!), tie some in a swag of greens for the front door, string them up as a garland, or let the kids glue a dot of glitter on the tip of each scale. The Victorians loved to make pinecones into Santas and other whimsical decorations.

Images of Father Christmas, Holly and Oak kings, Odin, Mother Berchta, Santa Lucina/Lucia

2

IMBOLC/BRIGID/CANDLEMAS
(February 1–7)

A drop of water. The ice lets go of one drop and then another, the near-freezing trickle becoming a small stream in the snowy mountains, which in turn becomes a river, the drop joining its brethren on the journey to the sea. Where it all began, the snow flutters down once again . . . .

When I think of Imbolc, I always think of white. White snows covering the tiny grasses and crocus flowers, pale poinsettias left from Yuletide festivities, long icicles and frozen ponds, and perhaps most important for this holiday, the white milk and cheese gained from the mothers of the first baby animals of the year.

Imbolc literally means "in the belly," suggesting both the world inside the belly of the Mother, about to be reborn into spring, and all kinds of animals that are also about to be born. Whether from cows, goats, reindeer, or any number of other domestic mammals, milk was a vital source of protein in the harsh winter months. Nowadays we have supermarkets to supply us with any kind of food we could wish for in the dead of the year, but our ancestors depended on both the milk and meat provided by the new calves, kids, lambs, and others.

Purification is a perfect theme for this holiday as well. The month of February's name comes to us from the ancient Roman festival of Februa, which was for purification and held in the middle of the month. The date of the Christian Candlemas (February 2) was determined by Jewish law—forty days after the birth of an infant it must be presented at the temple, and February 2 is forty days after Christmas. So the popular Pagan Februa festival became the Christian Candlemas after a change of date, name, and purpose.

Purification rituals would be a good choice to help celebrate this holiday. I certainly think of pure white snows, untouched by the footprints of man or beast, and the innocence of babes when I think of Imbolc. You might use clean snow and rub it on your hands and face, or use stream water or distilled water to purify yourself, some tools, your altar, and so on.

Mixing Oil and Water

The less hardy (or less cold tolerant types, like me) might prefer a hot, steamy bath as part of a purification ritual. There are few things I relish more on a cold winter night than a fragrant bubble bath with only a single candle to light the room, and perhaps some incense or soft, meditative music as well. Whether your area features rain or snow when Imbolc shows her face, think of the pure waters washing away any negativity, such as anger, sorrow, depression, or anything else you wish to "wash right out of your hair" (to take a phrase from the musical *South Pacific*).

Divination is another activity that works well on long, dark nights and cold, wet days when you're cooped up in the house. You might even try pouring a little scented oil on top of your bath water, and letting your inner sight tell you what the future may bring, or try to interpret the patterns the oil makes on the water's surface. This kind of divination is a lot like dream interpretation—what the symbol means to you personally is what matters, not what some book says it means. For example, a book might say that snakes are a symbol of regeneration and change, but if you're terrified of snakes, you might perceive a snake-shaped swirl of oil as a warning of danger ahead. If you're not sure how to interpret what you see, let you mind wander until the message is received or think analytically what a particular image makes you think of, then think how it might apply to your current circumstances.

Spinning a Yarn

Simple meditation, even when you're not in a hot bath, is a relaxing and revealing practice on wet days. Traditional wintertime activities years ago would have included spinning yarns, but I don't mean telling stories (although that's another fun seasonal activity). With a little practice and patience, you can make your own yarn using a spindle whorl or drop spindle. It's a very meditative activity, since you're using very little of your mind's attention to make the spun animal hair into yarn, espe-

cially when you get even a little proficient. The spindle turns and spins, creating a natural unfocussing focus—that is, by watching the spinning shape you can become mildly entranced and allow your mind to relax and wander.

All you need to make yarn in this way is a spindle whorl, a 12-inch bit of yarn or string for a leader, and some long-fiber "top," or combed wool. You can use any animal fiber you like to begin with, but those with long strands are easier to learn with. Tie the yarn leader onto the spindle where the stick goes through the disc of the whorl. Loop the yarn down under the whorl, make

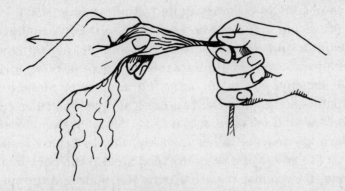

a half twist, come back up to the top of the stick, make another twist, and then tie a loop in the end. Draw out a bit of your yarn top, feed it through the loop in the string, lay it back on itself, and twist it together with your fingers. You're ready to begin spinning.

Now the trick is to spin the whorl clockwise with your right hand while holding the spun yarn in your left and drawing out new fibers with your right (reverse if left-handed). Give the whorl a twist, hold the twisting fibers in your left pinky and ring fingers, and pinch off the twist with your left thumb and forefinger. Between these fingers and your right hand, draw out some of the fiber a little at a time and release the twist up into the new fibers by letting the yarn slide down through your right hand.

Yes, your first yarn will be a lumpy mess and break off frequently—all beginners start off this way. Don't get discouraged! Simply keep practicing and draw out your fibers evenly to make even yarn. You'll soon learn how much is too much (this makes lumps, or "slubs") and how much is not enough (the yarn will become too thin and break). To correct a break, tease out the ends, add more new fiber, and begin spinning again carefully until you're past the break. When your spindle reaches the floor, unloop the yarn, wind it around the spindle, and twist on a new half knot at the top. As you become more practiced, you'll soon be able to twist the half knot, gauge the amount of fiber you need, and spin even yarn automatically. This is when you can let your mind wander and become only semiconscious of what your hands are doing.

When your spindle becomes quite full and heavy, you'll need to unwind it. Place your spindle in an empty box so that it can flip around as you unwind it and not roll across the room picking up hairs and playful cats. If you want an accurate measurement of how much yarn you've made exactly, you might want to purchase or make a "niddy noddy," which is something like two offset dowels on either end of a stout dowel. You wind the yarn onto it as you unroll it from the spindle. I use my yarn for weaving rather than knitting, so I don't really keep track of what I've got—I just wrap my yarn around the back of a chair. Once you have a large loop of yarn around the chair and the spindle is empty, clip the end/beginning of the yarn off the leader and grab the bundle of yarn with both hands on opposite sides of the chair. Twist the bundle up as tight as you can into a sort of "rope", then fold it in half and let it twist back on itself, making a "skein." This will hold everything in place until you're ready to set the twist.

Boil a large quantity of water and place your yarn skeins in the water. Boil them for about 5 minutes, then take them outside to dry. Untwist the skeins so you're back to your oval "chair loop" of yarn and place one end over a sturdy branch. On the bottom of the loop hang a weight, such as a half-filled milk jug, and allow the yarn to dry completely. You've set the twist and made your first one-ply yarn!

Candle Making

Making craft items, especially useful ones, is a good way to pass the dreary days while you're waiting for spring to arrive, something your ancestors did out of necessity. Candles are especially appropriate to make on Candlemas, which is the day many Christian churches, especially Catholic, bless all the candles to be used during the coming year, a tradition started in early medieval times.

Candles are surprisingly easy to make, contrary to what most people think—I believe people who have never made candles are the ones who say it's difficult to do. You need only an old saucepan or double boiler, some wax, some premade wick clips, and a mold. (Complete instructions for making candles are given below.) All you do is melt the wax, place a wick clip in the bottom of a pint or quart milk carton, and pour in the wax. Let the thing cool, and hey presto, you have a perfectly wonderful candle. Toss in a crayon for some color while the wax is melting.

If you want to get fancy, you can make dipped tapers, use commercial molds, pour in a bit of candle scent or essential oils, paint the finished candles, make gel candles . . . whatever! There are many books on the market with hundreds of candle-making ideas. It's a very fun craft and so easy that I actually taught myself to make them when I was in grade school. Just be careful when heating the wax, and let your imagination run wild. You can even get kits in a rainbow of colors for making candles out of rolled-up beeswax sheets if you don't want to be melting wax in your kitchen. There is no excuse for a coven to be buying all their candles when the things are so dead easy for anyone, even children, to make.

A Bit About Brigid

It's no accident that the making and blessing of the candles occurs on St. Brigid's day, and it's no accident that there happens to be a Celtic goddess by the name of Brigid. She is also called "the bright one" and "brightest arrow," an obvious allusion to her role as the maiden light-bringer, and she is sometimes pictured with a crown of candles. Until late in the eighteenth century, a shrine with an undying flame was kept in Kildare in Brigid's honor, nineteen nuns serving as priestesses to the Lady of the Flame. Besides being the light maiden, Brigid is also goddess of smithcraft, another fire association. If you can manage it, a particularly effective element for a Brigid ritual would be to get a real blacksmith to make small tokens (S-hooks, nails, etc.) for participants to take home. Have an anvil, forge, and barrel of water all set up with a coal fire burning hotly when everyone arrives—they'll be talking about it for years!

Snow Snakes

Another fun winter-time activity is to throw snow snakes. We're not talking about flinging some albino pet shop purchases—these snakes are made of wood and glide on snow or ice. This Native American game, played all over Canada and eastern America wherever there's snow, has several variations on both the location and the stick that's used. In some, the slightly tapering stick is an average of three feet long, highly polished for maximum glide, and is ornamented with a carved snake head at the larger front end. In others, the polished stick is more flat, almost like a miniature modern ski with a less curved tip, and is painted with decorations on the top side.

This is great fun for two or more players. If you don't have a wood-carver in your group that can make enough snakes for everyone, find old skis at thrift stores and flea markets and paint them however you like so you can tell them apart. The stick or ski is launched like an underhand javelin and sent sliding across the ice or snow. You can give it a running start and stop at a line drawn in the snow or give it a standing start. If you don't have a frozen pond handy, a level patch of clean snow (like a road or other bush-free track) works well too. In one variation, a lightly compacted track or groove is made in the snow for the snake to follow—this is probably the best technique if your snow is too soft to form a good crust and the snakes keep getting stuck.

As with most Indian games, wagers would be made on the outcome of challenges, either by the participants or by those watching on the side. The stick can go surprisingly far in ideal conditions (over two miles!), so the game is also great exercise unless you can train your dog to bring the snakes back or plan to just leave them until a future expedition down that direction.

Potting Spring Seeds

After so much winter, it feels so good to start getting ready for spring! The candles have been made, the days are getting longer, the seed orders have arrived, and now it's time to start planting. If you welcomed in the young Green Man for your ritual, a perfect activity for your group during or after the ritual is to plant spring seeds in pots. You can use new clay pots or cleanly scrubbed old ones with that nice "used" patina on the outside. Get several packets of easy-to-grow plant seeds, some fresh soil, and let your guests mix and match as they like. Some good choices to ensure that everyone has something that will actually come up later are marigolds, dwarf cosmos, coleus, tomatoes, bush beans, zinnias, sweet peas, and dwarf sunflowers.

If you're an avid gardener, this is the perfect opportunity to have your friends help you plant the early starts of your vegetable garden. Get everything prepared in advance (clear off a sunny windowsill, set the six-packs and other pots in trays, evenly distribute the soil in the pots . . . you know the drill) and give each person one packet of seeds and the appropriate number of pots. Put Mary in charge of the tomatoes, Andy in charge of the beans, Bob in charge of the cucumbers, Lisa in charge of the squash, and before you know it, all your veggie seeds will be ready to go. It's great fun to chat together over a warm cup of something while you're sharing this activity with your guests, perhaps imparting a little gardening knowledge at the same time. If your home and garden are the usual ritual location, it's both fun and satisfying for your coveners to see how "their" plants are coming along and finally pick the produce at a harvest ritual later in the year.

CRAFTS

Imbolc Stitchery

A silver candlestick in the form of a triple spiral supports three candles to represent the light's return to the world. This design features both metallic threads and rayon fibers for extra texture. (For additional stitchery instructions, see pages 211–214.)

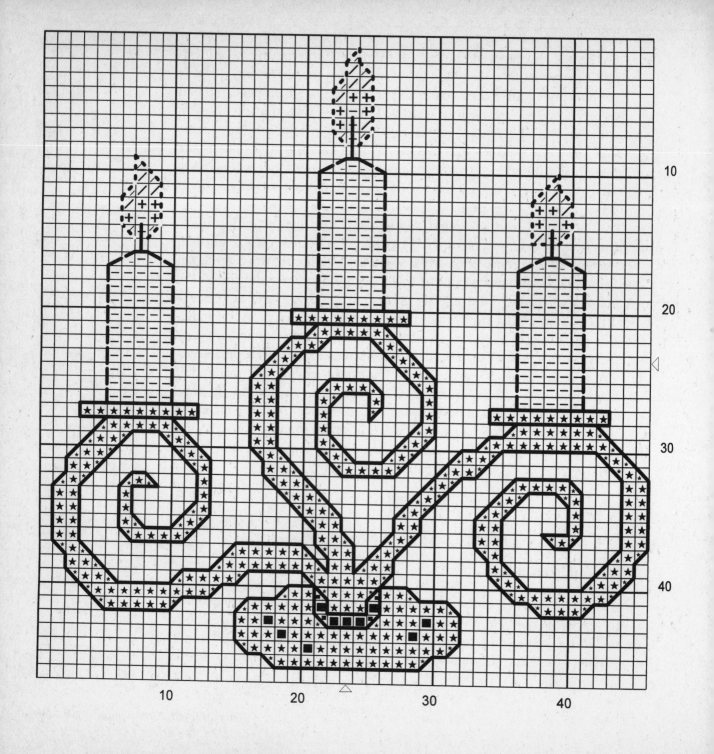

Grid Size:	47 W × 47 H
Cloth Count:	18
Fabric:	White Aida
Design Area:	2.61″ W × 2.61″ H

Pattern Key

Symbol	DMC Floss		Color
■	535	(2 strands)	Ash gray, very light
+	307 + Kreinik 091	(2 strands)	Lemon & Star yellow
/	444 + Kreinik 091	(1 strand)	Canary-bright & Star yellow
–	5200	(1 strand)	Snow white

Symbol	Kreinik		
★	001HL Silver #4 Braid	(1 strand)	

Backstitches

Symbol	DMC Floss	Color
——	310 (1 strand)	Black
---	535 (2 strands)	Ash gray, very light
....	972 (1 strand)	Canary-deep

Ice Candles

I can't think of a more symbolic candle to make on this holiday than ice candles. The secret to success on these is to use two different melt-temperature waxes, and to use extra cold ice—if your ice cream is so hard you need a jackhammer to get it out of the carton, your freezer is perfect for the kind of ice that makes great ice candles. You can, however, get satisfactory results from just one kind of wax if you want to avoid the extra hassle. Be sure to have on hand a box of baking soda or a fire extinguisher rated for grease first—just in case.

YOU'LL NEED:

Old double boiler pan or coffee can and old saucepan
2 pounds low-temperature paraffin or beeswax (120°F)
2 pounds high-temperature paraffin or beeswax (140°F)
2 colors of candle dye or wax crayons
Milk carton or other large-diameter candle mold
Candle wicking (not string!) or 4-inch wick clips for small candles
Mold putty
Mold release spray (if using a commercial mold)
Pencil or stick
Ice cubes
Ice pick
Sharp knife for trimming excess wax

While your double boiler is heating, cut the low-temperature wax into chunks (I use a flat-head screwdriver and a hammer) and place them in the top section, adding the dye of your choice. Allow the water in the bottom to just boil, and don't leave the room until you've finished making your candle. If the wax becomes overheated and catches fire, put it out with handfuls of baking soda or a fire extinguisher.

While you're waiting for the wax to melt, prepare your mold. Place the wick through the hole in the bottom of the mold or use the ice pick to make a hole if you're using a milk carton. Knot the wick and apply a blob of mold putty to seal the hole completely (modeling clay will melt, don't use it). If using a commercial candle mold, spray the inside of it with the release spray, coating it evenly but not thickly. Tie the wick to the pencil, making it tight enough that when the pencil rests on the top of the mold the wick is taut and straight. For a super simple variation on this, use a one-pint milk carton and set a 4-inch wick clip in the bottom—the top of the finished candle won't look as tidy, but there's no messing about with mold putty and wicking this way.

When the wax is completely melted, stir it a bit to ensure the dye is completely mixed in. Working quickly, pour the ice cubes into the mold, keeping the wick as straight and centered as possible. Immediately pour the wax into the mold, pouring any excess wax into another heatproof container for future use. Allow to cool completely. Pour out all the water left from the melting ice and shake the candle. If you hear trapped water, use the ice pick to gently poke a hole in the bottom of the wax chamber it's trapped inside and pour it out.

Using the same process, melt the high-temperature wax and dye. Pour this hotter second color of wax over the first and tap the mold to ensure the second wax has penetrated all the holes in the first wax. Pour any excess wax into a separate storage container for future use, then label the two containers so you can keep track of their different melt temperatures. Allow the candle to cool completely, remove it from the mold (if you used a milk carton, tear it off) and trim the ends of the wick before use. If the bottom of the candle is jagged, trim with a sharp knife.

Recycled Chunk Candles

Reduce, reuse, recycle! If you're as bad a packrat as I am (I'm getting better, I swear!), you save the larger bits of wax left over once your candles have burned down almost completely. This project is the perfect way to recycle those colorful leftovers into one lovely candle to honor the Divine.

YOU'LL NEED:

Old double boiler or coffee can and old saucepan

2 pounds paraffin or beeswax

Candle dye or wax crayons (optional)
Milk carton or other wide candle mold
Candle wicking (not string!) or 4-inch wick clips for small candles
Mold putty
Mold release spray (if using a commercial mold)
Pencil or stick
Assorted chunks of colored candle wax
Sharp knife for trimming excess wax

Follow the instructions under *Ice Candles* above for melting your wax and preparing the mold. Clean the candle leftovers so that there won't be any bits of old wick, herbs, stray insects, or other little gray things to make your new candle look dirty. Fill the mold with the colored wax chunks and blobs, making sure the wick stays centered and straight and mixing the colors so that they form a nice random pattern. Pour in the liquid wax, tapping the mold to make sure there won't be any trapped air bubbles. Allow to cool completely, remove from the mold, and trim both ends of the wick and bottom if necessary before use.

Etched Glass Candleholder

Fire and "ice" are combined in this project, where a votive or tealight flame is seen through a clear glass holder decorated with frosty motifs. Choose any designs you like—I've included several to select from that evoke images of the holiday.

YOU'LL NEED:

Glass candleholder (preferably straight-sided)
White adhesive-backed shelf paper
Carbon paper or pen
Sharp craft knife (such as an Xacto knife)
Cotton swabs
Glass etching paste

Begin by cleaning the holder thoroughly with glass cleaner or ammonia. Dry completely. Cut a piece of shelf paper to cover the entire surface you want to etch plus a little extra. Select a design you like and use carbon paper to trace it onto the paper, or draw one freehand with a pen. Carefully peel off the backing paper and stick the shelf paper onto the glass, starting from one end or from the center and smoothing it with your fingers as you work to avoid any bubbles. Use the knife to cut along the outline of the design and remove the paper from the area you want to etch.

With cotton swabs, spread the glass etching paste generously over the open areas of the pattern, being careful to keep it off your skin (it is acid paste and will burn) and within the boundaries of your shelf paper so you don't accidentally etch other spots on your glass. For an even frosted effect, there should be no gaps in the paste. Wait about five minutes, then wash off the paste under running water. The acid is neutralized by the water, so you can carefully use your hands to help remove any excess paste. Peel off the shelf paper and use a little glass cleaner to make your new holder shine.

Candle Crown and Linen Hair Cover

Spectacular to behold in ritual, the crown of candles is worn by a priestess representing Brigid, St. Lucia, or Lucina. Scandinavian countries have an annual festival on December 13 where a young girl is chosen to be Santa Lucia and wears the candle crown in a procession. It's obvious to Pagan eyes that this young girl is the Maiden bringing light back to the world after the depths of the long, cold winter have passed by. Traditional Lucia crowns have anywhere from four to nine candles, but I've designed this one with eight to represent the Wiccan wheel of the year. Most Lucia crowns now use battery-operated candles for safety (see Resources); please use good judgment when considering who will be wearing this crown with real candles.

YOU'LL NEED:

8 wooden candle cups
Drill
1/8-inch drill bit for wood and metal
White, green, or gold acrylic craft paint

½-inch flat brush
Steel or brass flashing or craft metal
Tin snips
100-grit sandpaper
Glue gun and glue sticks
8 metal screws and nuts, ⅛-inch diameter × about ⅜-inch long (total thickness of metal and wooden cup plus ¹⁄₁₆ inch)
8-inch white hook and loop tape, ½-inch wide
1 yard white muslin or linen
3½ yards white and gold "rope" trim, ¼-inch diameter
Scissors
Tacky fabric glue

Drill an ⅛-inch hole in the side of each wooden candleholder. Paint the holders and allow to dry completely. While the paint's drying, cut a 20-inch × 1¼-inch strip from the metal using tin snips, gloves and extreme caution to avoid getting cut on the very sharp edges. Still wearing gloves, sand all edges and corners of the metal until they are dull enough to be handled safely. Drill eight ⅛-inch holes in the metal, spacing them evenly and centering them along the strip. *Tip:* Clamp the metal strip to a scrap of wood to drill your holes. Gently bend the strip into an oval shape, working your way back and forth along the length of it slowly so you don't get any kinks.

Make a circle of hot glue around the edge of one of the holes in the metal, quickly laying a wooden cup on the glue and lining up the drilled holes. Hold the cup in place until the glue has solidified. Thread a screw from the inside of the metal oval through the candle cup, then place the nut on the end of the screw inside the cup and tighten it. Tighten the nut enough to hold the cup securely but not so tightly that you risk splitting the wood. Repeat until all eight candle cups are in place.

Separate the halves of the hook and loop tape. Generously hot glue a 3-inch length of the hook half to the inside back edge of the crown, hook side facing toward the metal and extending past it 5 inches. Generously hot glue a 3-inch length of the loop side on the outside of the crown, loop side facing the metal and extending past it 5 inches. This will securely fasten the ends of the crown and make it adjustable to fit any size head. If you're having trouble getting the glue to hold on the metal, try sanding it with 60-grit sandpaper or using a couple of metal screws and nuts per side to hold the tape in place.

To make the hair cover, cut a 36-inch circle from the muslin. Use fabric glue to attach the rope trim all along the edges of the muslin circle and allow to dry completely. To wear it, find where the ends of the trim meet and place that in the back. Place the circle off center on the wearer's head so that the trim forms a lovely wavy edge over her face and the majority of the cover trails down her back. Fit the crown over this covering tightly and both will be held in place.

Use cut-down tapers or "emergency" candles, which are slightly smaller in diameter and height, in the candle cups. Use a blob of candle "stickum" in the bottom of each cup for a secure fit and try to keep the period of use as brief as possible to avoid an excess of dripping wax. Fit the candles in place before placing the crown on the wearer's head. Another tip is to prelight the candles briefly and then blow them out so that they will be easier and faster to light later during your presentation.

Knotwork Print Block

The Goddess Brigid, being primarily an Irish deity, is celebrated here with a knotwork wooden block you can use to print anything from paper to fabric to each other.

YOU'LL NEED:

6-inch-square piece of ³/₄-inch-thick pine board
Carbon paper
Assorted wood or linoleum block cutting gouges
12-inch-square piece of acrylic or tempered glass
Assorted inks, fabric paints, craft paints, etc.
Rubber brayer
Paper or fabric to print on

Transfer the pattern provided or one of your choice onto the wood with the carbon paper. If you use your own pattern, remember that the

printed image will be a mirror image of what is carved into the block. If it makes the process easier for you, use a pencil to color in the areas that you will not be carving away. Use the largest U-gouge to remove the background, always carving away from your pattern so that if you slip you won't ruin the design. Also carve away from your hands and fingertips to avoid injury—use a clamp if necessary to help hold the wood steady while you work. When the background is finished and well below the level of the design, begin using smaller gouges to work the details. Take your time and work carefully—one slip can seriously mar the design.

When the woodcut is done, prepare your other materials, find a solid table to work on, and place cardboard behind any fabrics you are going to print. Pour a small amount of paint or ink onto the acrylic sheet and evenly coat the rubber brayer with it, running the roller back and forth through the paint. The brayer should be lightly covered, not gloppy or drippy. Gently and carefully roll the brayer over the wood block, evenly coating the design with a thin but opaque layer of paint. Now pick up the block and lay it down carefully on the spot you want to print, pressing down firmly without rocking or pounding the block. Carefully pull up the block and allow your print to dry.

If you will be using the block a lot, you might want to attach a simple cabinet knob or handle to the back to make it easier to handle. In that case, lay the block in a piece of foam with a bit cut out for the handle or simply hold it in your hand when you want to ink it up.

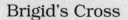

Brigid's Cross

Although wheat weaving is usually thought of as a harvest-time activity, these simple equal-armed crosses are a traditional decoration associated with Brigid. This project can actually be made with any kind of grasses if their stems are long enough, including oats and other grains, and decorative dried grasses used for arrangements.

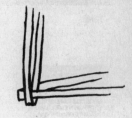

YOU'LL NEED:

Wallpaper soaking tray
Up to 36 wheat straws, heads attached
Wheat-colored embroidery floss
Scissors

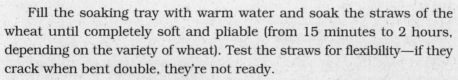

Fill the soaking tray with warm water and soak the straws of the wheat until completely soft and pliable (from 15 minutes to 2 hours, depending on the variety of wheat). Test the straws for flexibility—if they crack when bent double, they're not ready.

Begin the cross by folding one straw in half and slipping a second straw crosswise into the bend. Fold this second straw in half so that you now have two folded and interlocked straws making an **L**. The third straw should be folded in half to encompass both halves of the second straw, and the fourth straw should do the same to the third straw. You should now have four straws that are folded in half and meet in the center to form an equal-armed cross. Keep building up the "arms" by going around the shape clockwise, folding straws and laying them over the previous ones. Keep the arms flat and lay the straws next to each other—try using beanbags or some other soft weight on the ends to keep the arms in place as you work.

Use the floss to tightly tie off each arm just under the wheat heads. If the wheat has very large heads and/or very long beards, you can trim off the beards neatly, trim out some of the heads, leave just one head per arm, or trim off all the heads.

MENU

Assorted Cheese Platter

Winter Greens With Feta

Homemade Cream of Potato Soup

Buttermilk Loaf With Fresh Herbed Butter

Coconut Extra-Moist Angel Food Cake

Milk, Soy Milk

Assorted Cheese Platter

Cheese is perhaps the perfect party food, and this tray of bounty is more than just colorless cubes with toothpicks stuck into them. It's fun to go on a cheese scavenger hunt in your favorite gourmet food store—see how many exotic varieties you can find to entice your guests.

12	ounces extra-sharp white Cheddar	8	ounces smoked mozzarella (or your choice of smoked cheeses)
12	ounces marbled jack/Colby	12	ounces assorted gourmet hard cheeses
8	ounces pepper jack		

Slice each type of cheese about ¹/₂-inch thick. Using assorted canapé cutters, one shape for each type of cheese, cut shapes out of the cheese, nestling the cuts together as closely as possible to minimize waste. Arrange the various cheeses on a platter with a cup of party toothpicks in the center. Cover with foil or plastic wrap until ready to serve. Makes about 12 servings.

Winter Greens With Feta

If you're in a southern location or can protect your winter crops well enough with cold frames, you may be able to pick these cold-season greens right from your garden. Naturally, the feta is another nod to the first milks of the season.

1 cup baby spinach leaves

1 cup frisee (lacy French endive), coarsely torn into pieces

1/2 cup red or rainbow-colored chard, coarsely chopped

1/2 cup beet greens, coarsely chopped

1/2 cup radicchio, coarsely chopped

1/2 cup baby corn salad/mache leaves

1/2 cup baby dandelion greens

1/4 cup baby arugula leaves

1/2 cup red kale, finely chopped (not "flowering" kale)

1/2 cup feta cheese, crumbled

1/2 cup plain or glazed walnuts, chopped

Oil and vinegar or other light dressing

Toss the first eight ingredients in a large bowl until blended. Serve in individual bowls and top with a little of the red kale, crumbled feta, and walnuts. Drizzle the dressing of your choice over the salads (use a lightly flavored dressing so that you don't overpower the delicate flavors of the greens and feta). Makes about 6 servings.

Homemade Cream of Potato Soup

White and creamy but never boring, serve this comfort food with a fresh herb garnish and your guests will be talking about it for a long time to come.

1 tablespoon olive oil

1 small or 1/2 large onion, minced

4 cloves or 2 teaspoon chopped garlic

2 14 1/2-ounce cans vegetable broth

4 medium red potatoes, cubed

1 large or 2 small parsnips, cubed

1 tablespoon fresh sage, minced

Salt and pepper to taste

1/2 cup milk or cream

Sage leaves for garnish

In a large saucepan, heat olive oil. Sauté onion until just transparent, then add garlic and cook 1 more minute. Add vegetable broth, potatoes, parsnips, sage, and salt and pepper. Simmer until the vegetables are soft. Purée in a blender until smooth, return the soup to the pot, and add the milk. Heat again until serving temperature but do not boil. Serve hot with a sage leaf garnish and buttered bread on the side. Makes about 4 servings.

Buttermilk Loaf With Fresh Herbed Butter

These more subtle additions to the Imbolc menu still use dairy foods but with completely different results. The soft white bread with a fine, moist crumb is absolutely sublime by itself, and especially wonderful dipped in Homemade Cream of Potato Soup, with or without the herbed butter.

FOR THE BREAD:

1 tablespoon yeast	1 teaspoon salt
1/3 cup hot water	1 cup buttermilk
1 tablespoon sugar	About 2 1/2 cups white flour

FOR THE HERBED BUTTER:

1 cup heavy cream, preferably room temperature	1 teaspoon salt
1 tablespoon finely minced herbs, any combination: chives, rosemary, sage, thyme, oregano, fennel, parsley, savory, tarragon, basil, etc.	

To make the bread, combine the yeast and hot water in a small bowl and set aside until the yeast is softened. In a large bowl, combine the sugar, salt, and buttermilk. Add the yeast and water, stirring until blended. Add the flour a cup at a time, adding more if needed to make a good dough that pulls away from the sides of the bowl cleanly. Turn the dough out onto a well-floured surface and knead it for about 10 minutes, using as much flour as needed to keep it from sticking to the table and your hands. Allow to rise until doubled (about 45 minutes) in an oiled bowl covered with a clean cloth. After the dough has risen, punch it down and form it into an elongated oval (it will spread out flat a bit when baked, so make it as tall as possible), then transfer it to a nonstick or oiled cookie sheet. Make a single shallow slice down the middle of the loaf with a very sharp knife, and allow it to rise again (about 45 minutes) under the cloth. Remove the cloth and bake at 350 degrees F. for about 35 minutes or until the loaf is well browned and sounds hollow when tapped with your fingernail.

To make the butter, pour the cream into a clean glass jar with a tightly fitting lid. Shake the jar until the fat globules congeal into a single buttery hunk and the buttermilk is a completely separate liquid. This is a great activity for a group since everyone likes to take a turn at shaking the jar. Pour out the buttermilk (save it for other recipes) and push your freshly made butter out flat on a clean cloth. Run this under cold water, kneading it as necessary to wash out any remaining buttermilk and pat dry. Sprinkle the salt and herbs over the flattened butter and roll it up, then knead it a few times with your hands to distribute the seasonings evenly. Form whatever shape of butter pat you like and serve immediately or chill for later use.

Coconut Extra-Moist Angel Food Cake

Be prepared to give out copies of this recipe. Many, many copies. And did someone say snow? Try garnishing the top of this winter wonderland with miniature pine trees and skiers, giant snowflakes, or a snow family.

1½	cups sugar	1½	teaspoon cream of tartar
1	cup cake flour	1	teaspoon vanilla extract
1½	cups egg whites (about 18 small eggs)	1	teaspoon almond extract
½	teaspoon salt	1½	cups finely grated coconut
			White frosting of your choice

Preheat oven to 350 degrees F. Sift ¾ cup of the sugar and the flour together and set aside. Beat the egg whites until foamy, then add the salt and cream of tartar. Continue beating until the whites form stiff peaks. Gently beat in the remaining sugar, the extracts, and ½ cup of the coconut. Gently fold the flour mixture into the whites and pour into an ungreased angel food or tube cake pan. Bake for about 40 minutes until the top just begins to brown and the cake springs back when touched.

Cool completely upside down, supporting the pan on a bottle if the top has risen above the edge of the pan. Use a serrated bread knife to gently cut the cake away from the sides and bottom of the pan. Remove from pan, frost, sprinkle with coconut, decorate as desired. Makes about 8 servings.

DECORATIONS

Ice sculptures: An absolutely spectacular and memorable decoration for your table is an ice sculpture, so appropriate for winter gatherings. You can make them easily by simply using large candle molds, or if you have a bit of skill as a carver you can purchase a block of ice and have at it with some chisels and gouges. These are great to set in the center of a large punchbowl or an outdoor altar if the temperature is below freezing. Another idea is to freeze a plastic bowl full of water with a small cup in the center, then to remove the bowl and cup and place a lit candle in the center.

Snowflakes: Remember making cut paper snowflakes when you were a kid? They're every bit as much fun to make now, and if you have children of your own this is a great activity for a rainy or snowy afternoon. Make them in all shapes and sizes and plaster the windows with your creations or hang them from the ceiling from threads. Tissue paper 3-D "honeycomb" snowflakes are also available from party and classroom supply stores—they fold up compactly when not in use.

White flowers: Paperwhites are one of my favorite flowers! I love to have a pot of these fragrant little narcissius in my window to scent the house and lift my heart. You can grow paperwhites yourself or buy them at the nursery. White poinsettias, orchids, pansies, or any other seasonal white flower are all lovely decorations for Imbolc, and act as living reminders that spring is just around the corner during the dark days of winter.

Candles: Whether your candleholders are plain or ornate, clear glass or scrolls of metal leaves, candles and holders are another perfect accent for Candlemas. And of course, the candles themselves are part of the scene, whether scented confections that smell like cookies or a spring rain, floral shapes floated on bowls of water, or white glittery tapers surrounded by ferns to remind us of the Maiden and the Green Man. Since this is also the holiday of first milks, burn a ghee lamp as well, using clarified butter as the fuel (inquire about the supplies for these in Indian markets).

Knotwork: The Celtic connotations of Brigid, one of the most prominent deities of the day, are "knot" to be ignored. Use warm cotton throws with Celtic designs to enhance the furniture, hang printed cloth wall-hangings over drafty windows or plain walls, stitch and display knot-work needlework pillows in the comfiest chairs, and wear your best torc or Celtic earrings for the occasion. There's nothing wrong with decorating the host as well as the house!

Baby animals: A very appropriate motif for Imbolc is that of baby lambs, calves, foals, and any other furry farm mammal that is coming into the world about now. Use some of your Easter lamb decorations on the table, have the children draw baby animals with crayon on vellum and hang them in the window, or make party favors out of cottonball sheep.

Images of Brigid, Lucina/Lucia, young maidens and boys, Hindu sacred cow figurines

3

OSTARA/SPRING EQUINOX

(March 20–23)

This is one of my favorite holidays for the simple reason that I love spring. I love the fresh breezes that sometimes carry the fragrances of flowers to me, I love daffodils and other spring flowers, I love the bright green grass that hides brightly colored eggs, and I love how the world seems to be waking up after a long sleep. The sun is bright, the flowers are dancing in the wind, and the dewdrops reflect like diamonds in the morning light. It makes you joyful just to be alive and experiencing such beauty!

Ostara is one of the few holidays to pass down to us relatively unaffected by Christian changes. The fact that it's named after the Germanic goddess Eostar (or Eostre, Ostara, Eostra—take your pick) and hasn't been changed into Saint Whoever Day is amazing in itself, but when you consider that her magic hare that lays eggs is still along for the ride, it's a downright miracle. Even the floating Sunday that Easter occurs on is based on our original holiday—it's the first Sunday after the first full moon after the spring equinox.

Eggs and chicks, baby animals, abundant flowers, the hare or rabbit that emerges from the underworld with lots of little ones in tow . . . these are all unmistakable images of life renewal that have remained the same for centuries. So go ahead and have that egg hunt and buy the commercial bunny decorations without guilt—they were ours first, after all.

Spring is a time to get things going! Crops and flowers need to be planted, baby animals need to be raised, and the house needs to be cleaned. As a gardener, I can't wait to start sowing the seeds for the vegetable garden and starting flowers in the cold frame. After so many long months of gray skies and chill temperatures, this is the moment I've held my breath for.

Getting Started With a Mini-Greenhouse

If you're in a northern climate that can't plant out for another month or if you have pests that will eat your seeds or young shoots before they get a chance to grow, start some seeds in a greenhouse or cold frame. A cold frame is easy to make out of some straw bales and an old sliding glass door. The one pictured in the first photo insert has been out in the weather for about four years and the straw bales are still fine (I nibbled away at the one on the right for my chicken nest boxes). Just remember to prop the window open on sunny days or you'll cook your seedlings. You can make a smaller cold frame out of just a sheet of clear plastic and a cardboard box, too.

Good vegetable crops to start the season off with include potatoes, radishes, spinach, peas, chard, beans, carrots, lettuces, and others that like cooler weather. Things like tomatoes and corn need a lot of heat and long days, so check any vegetable gardening book for suggestions on what to grow in your area in March and April.

Morris Dancing

The fields and gardens should be blessed before planting, and this is a perfect time to do just that, especially if you have others that want to participate. Morris dancing, believed to have originated from the Moorish ("Morris") people, is a traditional and extremely ancient way of "waking up the Earth" after winter is over in England and Wales. There are many, many variations on how the dance is done and what is used, from hankies to sticks to antlers to swords. Historically and to this day, morris dancing is also done on every holiday, including Yule, Imbolc, and Beltane. If you'd like more in-depth information on how traditional morris dancing is done, you're going to need to get a detailed book or contact a local troupe for a demonstration, but for our purposes we'll keep it very simple and quite nontraditional. The intent to drive away the last bits of winter and bless the fields is the important thing here.

Dress in bright colors and use lots of bells to help wake up the fields. There are instructions below for making simple ankle bells, and these are traditionally worn by morris dancers. You can either have everyone dance and jump around freeform, or you can practice a simple dance beforehand. Try something like "right foot stomp, left foot stomp, right foot stomp, twirl on the right foot, land on the left and stomp, hop." You might even want to add traditional morris sticks (1-inch dowels cut to about 14 inches long) and clack them together with a partner after each section of the dance. Make sure you're stomping and dancing outside the actual planting area, however, or you'll compact the soil, making it difficult to plant.

Blessing the Fields

There are many other ways to bless the fields as well. Those in the American Southwest might want to sprinkle blue corn meal over the land as a blessing, while those in grain-producing areas could use whole-wheat flour, or those from Asia could use rice or rice flour. (Do not use tobacco to bless your garden, since it can harbor the tobacco mosaic virus, which is deadly to tomatoes, potatoes, and some other vegetables.)

Of course, a particularly powerful fertility rite would be to make love in the fields before planting them. This can also be simulated with the traditional Great Rite wherein the High Priestess hold a chalice of wine (or salt water or milk or whatever liquid you feel is appropriate) and the High Priest holds the athame as it is plunged into the cup (there are many variations of what words the HPS and HP say here). The contents are then poured out upon the ground and the athame tip is placed inside the earth as well to bless the land.

If simply having a parade with musical instruments or kazoos or singing as you march deosil (clockwise) around the fields seems like a good way to bless your land, then go for it! It's the intention of waking up the land and blessing it that matters, not so much the technique. Don't forget about any sleepy fruit trees and other food-producing plants—make sure you honor them as well, or even the flower garden if you don't grow any kind of crops. Then later you can use the flowers from this blessed garden on your seasonal altar.

How's the Weather Outside?

Ostara is also a good time to put up a weather station. These can be made from expensive kits that include complicated equipment with unpronounceable names, or they can simply be a few things like a rain gauge, thermometer, and barometer. If you have an inquisitive mind, you'll love knowing exactly what the conditions are outside, and you may get quite good at predicting the weather based on your instruments. Unlike some people who think that religion and science are incompatible, I know that science furthers my appreciation for Mother Earth and how wonderfully complex the world is. I feel more in touch with the changes of the Earth when I know how cold or hot it is outside, whether the barometric pressure is going up or down, exactly how much rain we got last night, and how fast the wind is going. With so many people spending more and more time in their homes in front of the computer or working in windowless cubicles, it's good to have as many ways as possible to connect to nature.

Keeping Chickens

When we moved back to the country with my young son, one of the first things we did was get a couple of little chicks. The fluffballs were only two or three days old when we bought them at the feed store, and we had to keep them in the bathroom under a light for warmth. My son loved to hold them and let them walk all over his arms and head, and I loved how he was getting the experience of watching these chicks grow into the chickens that we get our eggs from.

In a world where most people buy all of their food at the grocery and don't know or don't care how the animals are treated that supply some of that food, it's important to teach our children about the origins of what they eat. As Pagans I believe we try harder to follow the rhythms of nature and understand these cycles, but how many of us have been to a farm? How many have held a chicken or milked a cow? Fewer still have butchered their own meat, and an even smaller portion have shown this to their children.

The cycle of life and death is what makes up the Pagan universe, and my small contribution to my son's understanding of this is to own chickens. He's seen them grow from little peeping chicks into colorful hens and has gathered and eaten the eggs that they've produced. If you can manage it where you live, get some very young chicks on Ostara and raise them in your yard. If you can watch them hatching on Ostara, perhaps by visiting a local farm or hatchery, all the better! They actually don't need very much care once their adult feathers have come in at about one month, and since each hen lays about 300 eggs a year, you don't need a whole flock to keep your family (and perhaps the neighbors) supplied with fresh, organic eggs continuously. (See Resources for suggested books on how to raise your own chickens.)

Equinox Egg Balancing

An interesting experiment that's perfect for Ostara is to balance an egg on end. Impossible, you say? Not on the exact equinox. This will actually work for up to an hour before and after the exact moment of the equinox, and will amaze your guests. Take a fresh egg and find a perfectly flat countertop or use a dinner plate. Wide end down, carefully balance the egg and it will stand upright until the equinox is over. There are some astronomers and Web sites that enjoy claiming this is not a genuine phenomenon, but I have done it myself with friends over the years many times and it really does work. Just be sure you know the exact time of the equinox in your time zone and have some patience, as variations in the shell can make any individual egg easier or more difficult to balance.

Encapsulated in the egg is one of the world's ancient mysteries—the mystery of where life comes from. How can something that appears to be dead, even rocklike, bring forth a live chick that's ready to take on the world? This is one of the aspects of nature that fascinated our ancestors and made the egg a popular symbol of rebirth, of spring, and of new life. It's still fascinating, even today, to watch a live animal work its way out of this apparently inanimate object. Even though we know there's something alive within the seamless shell, it's an exciting moment to see the egg wobble a bit, then slowly form a tiny crack, then begin to open from a small hole until a fragile new being comes into the world through its own strength and determination. And that's the heart of what Ostara is all about.

CRAFTS

Ostara Stitchery

The Easter . . . er . . . Ostara bunny has come to deliver a special message of renewal. Blended floss colors add extra texture to the rabbit's fur, and metallic threads give a lifelike look to the whiskers. (For additional stitchery instructions, see pages 211–214.)

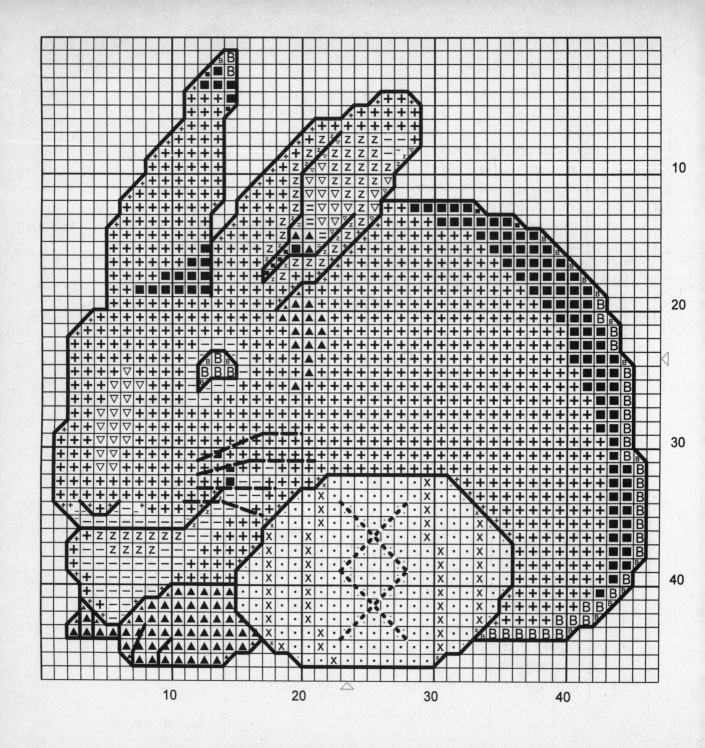

Grid Size:	47 W × 47 H
Cloth Count:	18
Fabric:	Pink Aida
Design Area:	2.61″ W × 2.61″ H (45 × 45 stitches)

Pattern Key

Symbol	DMC Floss		Color
B	310	(2 strands)	Black
+	613 + 840	(1 strand each)	Drab brown—very light & beige brown—medium
▲	840 + 301	(1 strand each)	Beige brown—medium & mahogany—medium
=	301	(2 strands)	Mahogany—medium
▽	3064	(2 strands)	Desert sand
Z	950	(2 strands)	Desert sand—light
–	822	(2 strands)	Beige gray—light
X	700	(2 strands)	Christmas green—bright
·	White	(2 strands)	White
■	840 + 310	(1 strand each)	Beige brown—medium & black

Backstitches

Symbol	DMC Floss		Color
——	310	(1 strand)	Black
- - -	231	(1 strand)	Christmas red

	Kreinik	
- - -	105C antique silver cord	

Royal Jewels Ostara Eggs

You'll have to keep reminding yourself that these are meant to be eaten! Decorate your hard-cooked eggs with any one of these colorful embellishments, or combine them for an amazing display of spring joy. This craft is especially popular with the kids.

YOU'LL NEED:

Hard-boiled eggs, any color
Tacky craft glue
Gold leaf, composite leaf, metallic foils
Rhinestones in assorted shapes and colors
Glitter, assorted colors
Metallic sequins, assorted shapes and colors
Metal jewelry charms, assorted shapes and colors
$^{1}/_{16}$-inch satin ribbons, assorted colors
$^{1}/_{8}$-inch satin ribbons, assorted colors

Ideally, your dyed or colored eggs should be as deep in color as possible for a real jewel-tone look. Excellent colors to shoot for are purple, royal blue, emerald green, rich aqua, burgundy, and red. Use acrylic craft paints if traditional dyes aren't getting the eggs as richly colored as you'd like—just be sure to let the paint dry overnight so you don't run into problems with the glue refusing to stick properly.

If using the gold leaf, tear it in small, random shapes and stick it right to the wet paint, allowing the paint color to show through between the pieces of leaf. Gently brush the finished egg with a light coat of thinned glue to ensure the leaf will stick and lay down nicely.

If you're using one particular type of decoration, such as rhinestones or charms, place them randomly all over the egg. If you're using glitter, make patterns with the glue like stripes, dots, intersecting lines to form diamonds, spirals, overlapping scales, and even pictures like bunnies or chicks. Ribbons can be run lengthwise or around the circumference of the egg and smoothed down carefully. To combine the techniques, use ribbons to separate areas and fill them in with sequins, perhaps adding a dot of glitter to the middle of each one. Or you could dye the egg sky blue, make green glitter "grass" on one end of the egg, and place metal fairy charms in the "air" to make a scene. Have fun with the materials and watch what the kids do—they'll come up with ideas you'll be surprised by.

Keepsake Painted Eggs

The eggshells are hollowed out before painting so that you can keep the results forever. You can use the whites and yolks in many recipes. Napkin rings can be used to elegantly hold the shells for display.

YOU'LL NEED:

Raw eggs
Ice pick or awl
Small bowl
Paper towels
Carbon paper (optional)
Clean used butter tub
Assorted acrylic craft paints
Assorted fine hair brushes, from size 1 down to 5/0 or smaller
Craft knife (optional)
Matte spray finish

Begin by selecting an egg without any surface flaws or bumps. Carefully pierce the narrow end of the egg with the ice pick to form a small hole. Carefully pierce the wide end of the egg with the ice pick, making a larger hole about 1/4 inch in diameter. Use the ice pick to scramble the insides of the egg a bit, breaking the yolk and separating any membranes so that the contents are easier to remove. Hold the egg over the small bowl and blow into the smaller hole very hard to remove the liquid egg. Rinse out the inside of the egg shell with water when you're done, shaking it firmly to clean out any last bits of egg, and allow to dry completely.

Now you can either trace a design you like onto the egg with carbon paper or paint it freehand. Try looking in gardening magazines for

Keepsake painted eggs: The egg on the left is from a cockatiel, on the right from an araucana hen.

things like small butterflies, flowers, hummingbirds, and so on to trace onto the egg. If freehanding, you may wish to lightly outline your design with a pencil first. Fill the butter tub with about 1 inch of water and reserve the lid for use as a paint palette. Pour a small dot of each paint color you'd like to use around the palette and set the dried egg shell on some towels to help hold it while you paint. Use the larger brush to fill in any large areas, and use smaller brushes to do detail work, like butterfly wings and such. Use a little dot of water on the palette as needed to thin the paint if you're having trouble with it drying too quickly or you can't get fine enough detail. If necessary, cut down a small brush with the craft knife until it's just a couple of hairs for extremely fine details. Allow each design to dry completely before starting on a new portion of the egg. When you're done, spray the shell with matte spray finish and display it out of the reach of small children.

If you choose to embellish the pots, make sure the paint has dried completely and the pots do not feel cool to the touch. If they feel distinctly cool, the paint's moisture has entered the porous clay but has not yet evaporated and may cause the glue to not stick properly. When you're sure the paint is dry, start gluing on your glitter, sequins, rickrack, fringe, or whatever else tickles your fancy. Allow to dry completely and then either display them as-is or fill them with silk or real spring plants (be aware that moisture may make some glued-on decorations come off over time).

Green Willow Baskets

Gather an armload of new willow stems and make one of these baskets for the egg hunt, or make one in advance for May Day. Remember to weave these as tight as you can because the stems will shrink as they dry.

YOU'LL NEED:

About 30+ green willow stems
Pruning shears
Raffia (optional)

To gather green willow stems that are good for weaving, look near streams and other wet places for where willow trees grow. Weeping willow stems will work fine for the weavers, but you'll need sturdy river willows for the spokes. Select long stems with only leaves on them and no little branchlets if possible. A few small branchlets near the top of the stem is okay. Cut them low down on the stem and leave an offering when you're done—a traditional Indian offering for gathered materials is to take some hairs from your head (it's only fair). Strip the leaves from the stems by starting at the thin end and running your fingertips backwards down to the base of the stem. Don't worry about trying to strip off any little buds, these will actually help you weave the basket later. Finish stripping off the leaves by taking off the last few at the tip of the stem or pinching it off if it's too wet and brittle to weave with. Separate your stems by size, selecting the seven thickest stems for the spokes of your basket.

Starting at the middle of each, lay six stems out on a flat surface, such as a patio or kitchen floor. Weave them over and under each other to form a square. Starting at the thin end, weave one of the thinner stems in and out of the spokes to help secure it, pushing the weave in toward the center as you hold the square in place. This is a difficult step, so take your time. When you get to where you started, add a seventh spoke by weaving it into the center square, then secure it with the thin weaver stem.

It doesn't matter if you weave clockwise or counterclockwise (most baskets are made counterclockwise, or from left to right), but if you want to make one for magical purposes you might take the direction of the weave into consideration. For example, you may want to weave one counterclockwise (widdershins), fill it with stuff you want to be rid of, then burn the whole affair. Alternately, you could weave one deosil and give it as a gift to someone you wish to be friends with a long time. Use your imagination.

When the first weaver becomes too thick to weave with, add in another starting at the thin tip end. To add a new weaver, follow the last weaver over and under a few spokes until it's secured, then drop the thicker weaver and weave only with the new thinner one. The thick ends of the weavers will be cut off later on the outside of the basket. Try not to add new weavers at the same point over and over—distribute them as equally as you can all over the sides for a stronger and more even basket.

When the basket is the diameter you like (my example, pictured in the first photo insert, is about 7 inches wide), gently bend the spokes upward at a 90-degree angle until they snap a little. The remaining half-stem and bark will keep the spokes in place, but you do need to be gentle with these hinged spokes until further weaving secures them. As you break the spokes, gather them up into a bundle in you nonweaving hand. Continue weaving in and out of the spokes, adding new weavers as needed. The bottom will probably be quite open, but don't worry— you're not making a museum piece and your first basket will probably be pretty funky, so just have fun with it.

At this point you may wish to trim off the tips of the spokes so they're not too ungainly, so trim them to about 14 inches long from the point they bend upwards. Use a rubber band to help hold the ends if you're having trouble keeping them in a bundle. Continue weaving in and out, adding new weavers as needed, but don't weave too tightly or you'll end up with a severely volcano-shaped basket. After about the fourth round of weaving on the sides of the basket, release the spokes and straighten them, pulling them upward through the weaving if needed to help correct an overly fat bottom. Push the weaving as far down the spokes as you can.

Continue weaving up the sides, pushing the wickerwork down tightly, straightening the spokes as needed, and correcting the overall shape. When the basket is about 4 inches tall, add the handle. I happened to find a red-stemmed willow growing next to my other weaving willows and thought it would make a pretty handle.

Select four more stems for the handle, and flip two of them around so that you have two butt ends and two tip ends on each side. Trim the bundle to about 30 inches long, making very sharp angled cuts at the ends. Firmly push one butt end and one tip end down next to a spoke until it reaches the base where the spoke is bent. Do the same with the other two ends next to an adjacent spoke. Twist the four stems together as tightly as you can to create an even, twisted handle, and push the stems down next to two adjacent spokes on the opposite side of the basket.

Continue weaving two or three more stems into the sides, treating the handles as one large spoke. To bend the weaver between the two branches of the split handle, place your fingertips on the very butt end of the weaver and curve it carefully around as shown to avoid breakage. End the last weaver at the handle and trim off the excess at an angle. Cut off any remaining butt ends and tips at an angle, making sure they are held securely in place by a spoke so they don't slip back inside the basket.

To make the rim, start with one of the spokes next to the handle. Bend it down at a 90-degree angle (it will probably break partially like at the bottom of the basket), let it lay naturally behind the next spoke, then tuck it in front of the second spoke over to hold it. Take the next spoke (the one the previous one just went behind) and do the same, continuing to tuck the ends of the spokes in front. When you reach the beginning, take the end and flip it under the bent spoke and in front of the second spoke, just like the others. Trim the ends at an angle, making sure they won't slip behind the spoke that's trapping them.

If you're not using it immediately, allow the basket to dry, then check the tightness of the handle. If it's loose and you'll be carrying it by the handle a lot, you may wish to wrap it securely with some raffia or other weaving material where it emerges from the rim of the basket.

Ankle Dance Bells

Wake up the Earth! Morris dancers use ankle bells sort of like an alarm clock while they dance to bring in the spring. Now you can do the same. This is a very popular activity with the kids too, so make extra sets to have on hand for young visitors.

YOU'LL NEED:

1/2-yard 1/2-inch-wide hook-and-loop tape, any color (red or green are good choices)

Scissors

Heavy button or quilting thread to match

Heavy embroidery or upholstery needle

12 silver or gold-tone 1-inch or 1 1/4-inch jingle bells

You'll need different sizes for children, women with dresses, men with pants, and so on, so make small, medium, and large ankle bells. Small is about 9 inches total length, medium is about 12 inches, and large is about 18 inches. For one set of ankle bells, cut the hook-and-loop tape to the length desired and separate the halves. Put them back together again with about 3 inches of hooks and loops extending past the ends of the connected halves. Form an open circle with the tape, making the exposed soft loop portion face toward the middle and the rough hook portion face away from the middle (this avoids scratched naked ankles and irritated guests). Run your fingers along the tapes where they are connected to smooth out any wrinkles on the inside of the circle.

With any kind of pen, pencil or marker, make six evenly spaced dots on the overlapping connected portion of the tape. Securely stitch a bell to each dot, going through both layers of tape and using plenty of thread as needed. Repeat for the other matching ankle bells so you have a pair. To wear them, use the exposed portions of tape to secure the bells to the ankles, strapping them on tightly and pressing the halves together firmly so the bells don't work loose while dancing.

Seed Packet Collage

Wait . . . what did we plant again? Rather than throwing out those used seed packages or stuffing a wad of them back in your cabinet "for future reference," make a colorful collage that will remind you what you've planted. You can even arrange them like a miniature garden so you can tell exactly what varieties will be coming up where.

YOU'LL NEED:

Opened seed packets, any kind with a picture
Small, sharp scissors like embroidery scissors
$8^{1}/_{2} \times 11$-inch posterboard
White glue or spray adhesive

Cut out each picture in an attractive manner, either leaving the image whole, cutting it into an interesting shape, or cutting around the outline of the object depicted. Pivot the picture you're cutting, not the scissors, to get a nice detailed cutting line. Arrange the images on a piece of paper without gluing them, overlapping the pictures so that you completely cover the board if possible, and placing larger, more complete images to the back, stand-alone objects to the front. When you're happy with the arrangement, glue the pictures one at a time to the posterboard in the same order, using very little glue and spreading it out with your fingers. Alternately, you can use spray adhesive to stick the images to the board.

Origami Rabbit Candy Box

These cute little bunnies, made from folded paper, are so fun to make they will multiply rapidly! (Check out one example in the first photo insert.) Have everyone make one to take home, use them as place settings for the table; hide them in the yard for the kids to find . . . the possibilities are endless.

YOU'LL NEED:

Origami paper
Assorted markers, fake whiskers, eyes, etc. (optional)
Jelly beans, bunny corn, other small candies

Begin by folding the paper in half, then half again. Unfold, then fold from corner to corner, and fold this in half again. Unfold—you will have four creases shaped like a star on your paper, and these will help you find where to make the next folds.

Fold your paper, colored side out, in half toward you so that it forms a rectangle. Take the top corners of this rectangle and bring them inside to the center line—you will be folding on the diagonal creases and forming a triangle. Take the two bottom corners of the triangle and fold them up to the top of the triangle, making a small square on top of the larger triangle. Fold the left and right corners of the small square in to the center of the square. Fold the two upper tips down over these last folds, then fold these in half again. Tuck the folds you just made into the pockets.

Turn the shape over, open end toward you. Fold the left and right sides into the center and toward you. Fold the two points that are nearest you at a 45-degree angle away from you and across the triangles you just made. Fold the corners closest to you back in to the center. Open up your bunny shape a bit, and give it "the breath of life"—blow into the hole until the shape puffs up. You may have to help it a little by gently tugging on the bottom and sides, and if you blow it up too much you can gently fold it on the sides to make a better rabbit shape. Decorate your bunny with a face and other features if you like. "Feed" the bunny with the candy until it's as full as you like.

Blow
Here

Baby Greens and Radishes With Strawberry Dressing

New Red Potato Salad With Egg

Baby Vegetables in Puff Pastry Eggs

Spun Sugar Nests

Assorted Fruit Juices

Baby Greens and Radishes With Strawberry Dressing

If you can't find 'Easter Egg' radishes in the store or your garden, use regular red radishes and cut little flowers into their skins to expose the white flesh beneath. The Strawberry Dressing adds just the right amount of sweetness and pinkness to the table.

4	cups assorted baby greens or mesclun salad mix	3/4	cup mushrooms, sliced
1	cup 'Easter Egg' radishes, cut into wedges	1/4	cup carrots, grated

FOR THE DRESSING

3/4	cup strawberry yogurt	1	tablespoon vinegar
2	tablespoons milk	1	teaspoon poppy seeds
2	tablespoons walnut or vegetable oil	1/2	teaspoon fennel or anise seeds
		1/4	teaspoon pepper (optional)

Layer all salad ingredients in a large bowl with the greens on the bottom and the radishes on top. Whisk together all dressing ingredients and toss with the salad or serve on the side. Garnish with edible flowers or sliced strawberries if desired. 6 servings.

New Red Potato Salad With Egg

New potatoes are very creamy and sweet, perfect for making this chunky salad. And what would Ostara be without eggs? This is my mother's recipe and is truly one of the best potato salads I've ever had.

8	small red potatoes, skins on, cut into large cubes	1	teaspoon salt
1/2	cup mayonnaise	1/4	teaspoon pepper
1/4	cup yellow onion, minced	1/4	teaspoon celery salt
1	tablespoon mustard	1/2	cup celery, chopped
1	teaspoon onion powder	3	hard-boiled eggs, coarsely chopped

Steam the potatoes until soft but not crumbly. While the potatoes are steaming, combine all remaining ingredients in a large bowl except the eggs. Add the potatoes to the mayonnaise mixture and mix until blended. Add the eggs, tossing gently to mix until blended. Chill for several hours before serving for best flavor. 6–8 servings.

Baby Vegetables in Pastry Eggs

Awwww! They're so cute! This dish is dedicated to all babies, including vegetable ones. Cut them small-scale to accentuate their petite size, but leave them large enough to be a nice mouthful too. When purchasing baby carrots, make sure they are true babies, not just full-sized carrots that have been put through a machine to make them into little nubs— these are pithy and will not cook properly.

FOR THE FILLING

4	baby crookneck or zucchini squash, washed and trimmed	1/2	cup snowpeas, sliced on the diagonal
1	cup baby carrots	1/2	cup enoki mushrooms, trimmed to 2 inches long
1	cup very small broccoli florets		
1	cup pearl onions, peeled, trimmed and halved	1	tablespoon parsley, minced
		1	teaspoon salt
1	12-ounce can baby corn (drained)	1/4	teaspoon black or white pepper

FOR THE CRUST

Pie crust recipe on page 176 (omit rosemary)

FOR THE GARNISH

½ cup Chinese hoisin sauce, chilled

Steam squash, carrots, broccoli, and onions until just tender but not soft. Carefully transfer to a colander and run under cold water immediately to stop the cooking. Set aside the squash, and place the carrots, broccoli, and onions in a large bowl. Add the corn, snowpeas, and mushrooms. Sprinkle parsley, salt, and pepper over the vegetables and toss gently to season them.

Preheat the oven to 400 degrees F. and lightly grease a cookie sheet. Divide the crust dough into four portions and roll each out into a rough circle. Lay one crookneck squash in the center of a dough circle, then pile a fourth of the other vegetables over it. Fold up the edges of the circle and begin pinching the dough together until you completely enclose the filling. Carefully flip this pocket over and place it on the cookie sheet, gently pushing it into an egg shape. Repeat for the other three pastry eggs. Bake for about 12–15 minutes or until the crust is a nice golden brown.

Just before serving, spoon the chilled hoisin sauce into a pastry bag with a medium lettering tip or into a condiment squirt bottle. Decorate the eggs with the hoisin sauce, making lines, dots, zigzags, and other designs just like you were decorating an Easter egg. You could also do this right at the table for an extra flashy show. Serve immediately. 4 servings.

Spun Sugar Nests

This recipe is relatively difficult, but after you get the technique down it gets much easier. Set aside some time in the morning to make the nests so you won't feel rushed, and store them in airtight containers until ready to use, preferably the same day for best results. In French cuisine, spun sugar is often piled on top of custards or ice cream, so if your nests look more like blobs, you can save the dish by serving the threads that way instead. In any event, it will be a dessert your guests will never forget.

1	cup sugar	Candy eggs
1/2	cup water	Marshmallow chicks
5	drops green food coloring (optional)	

In a small pan over high heat, combine the sugar and water, stirring until the sugar dissolves completely. Allow to boil for several minutes until the mixture begins to thicken. As soon as the sugar mixture begins to turn golden, pour it into another heatproof container, such as a glass measuring cup. Do not allow the mixture to cook further or it will become dark and taste burnt! If the mixture is still bubbling, put the cup in a shallow dish of cold water for about a minute to stop the cooking action.

To make the "angel's hair" candy, you'll need a nonstick cookie sheet and two forks. Place the cookie sheet on your kitchen table or a large

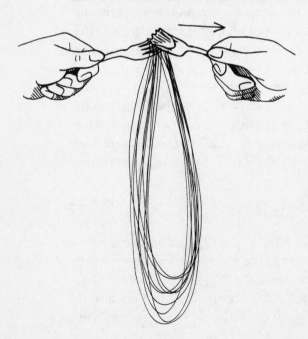

counter with the container of hot sugar mixture next to it on your right (if right-handed). In your left hand, hold one of the forks as if you were going to eat with it and hold it over the cookie sheet. Dip the other fork in the hot syrup, holding it the same way, and lay the tines on top of the other fork's tines. Blow on the syrup briefly, then pull the top fork away quickly but gently to form several thin strands of spun sugar candy. Pull away quickly to arm's length, then come back and touch the fork to the one in your left hand again.

Pull away again, and repeat until the syrup becomes too hard to form any more threads. Gently break off this bunch of threads and loop them into a small circle on a corner of the cookie sheet or on a separate sheet. Repeat this process, pulling out threads of spun sugar, at least five times per nest, coiling the resulting threads on top of the walls of the nest to build them up. Coil the threads immediately as they become brittle very quickly—don't try to make the threads ahead of time and coil them later. As you work, you may need to reheat the syrup slightly if it becomes too cool to form threads properly. Fill the center of each nest with three candy eggs and a marshmallow chick. Makes 4–6 nests.

DECORATIONS

Rabbits: What do rabbits have to do with Easter? Nothing. What do rabbits have to do with Ostara? Everything! We're lucky that the rabbit still has such a prominent place in decorations this time of year, and that many items featuring rabbits are available. If you have kids (or think like one), some cartoonish window decorations or silly egg cups might be in order, or you can place some sculpted naturalistic rabbits next to some flowers or houseplants for a more sophisticated look.

Baby animals: Fortunately, one aspect of Ostara that's shared with Easter is the motif of baby animals. Besides bunnies, we can easily find decorations featuring chicks, ducklings, lambs, and others for any situation, from garlands to dish towels, glassware to window clings.

Birds, nests, eggs: I love to collect old bird nests when I find them blown down in a storm or attached to a branch, abandoned after months or years. Be careful when handling bird nests if they look very fresh, for they can harbor disease-causing microorganisms—if you're not sure about their safety, use them outside only or spray them with a liberal coating of disinfectant and allow them to dry for a few days. Within these or manufactured nests found at craft stores, place tiny birds and eggs, adding a few little feathers for a finishing touch. Use birds all over the house in unexpected hiding places, whether from your craft store or your Yule tree ornament box. And eggs, dyed or plain, brown or white, should be mounded in baskets for the day, decorated, emptied of their contents and painted, or otherwise used wherever they will add a spot of interest.

Egg tree: A popular decoration for Easter has become the egg tree, which is usually a leafless, dried branch of manzanita or similar sculptural wood that has been left natural or painted white and mounted on a base. Blown eggs tied with ribbon, miniature wooden ornaments, or holiday decorations made by the children are hung from the branchlets for a festive tabletop display.

Flowers and plants: Naturally, any kind of plants, especially flowering ones, are essential for evoking a true feeling of spring. Live spring bulbs in pots add color, fragrance, and texture to any situation, indoors or out. Create a "color bowl" for your porch by planting spring bulbs and/or spring flowers in a large, shallow pot. Good selections would be assorted colors of crocus, grape hyacinth, pansies, and perhaps a head of ornamental flowering kale in the middle.

Flowering branches: A dramatic accent that many people don't think to use or know how to display well are the branches of flowering trees and shrubs. Forsythia, quince, cherry, apple, pussy willow, acacia, and many other beautiful branches look fantastic bundled in an antique bucket on the porch, clipped shorter and placed in bud vases Japanese style, or simply laid on and around the altar or buffet table.

Images of the Spring Maiden, Persephone, Eostre, Green Man

4

BELTANE/MAY DAY/ WALPURGIS

(April 30–May 6)

ove and sex? Is that all Beltane is good for? Well, yes and no. Admittedly we all greatly enjoy the love and sex part, but Beltane is also across from Samhain on the Wheel . . . the other time of the year when the Veil is thinnest. It's the time when faeries visit our gardens and the spirits of future babies (both human and animal) come over from the Summerland where they've been resting and waiting. My own son was conceived on Beltane as I opened myself up to the Goddess energies and my husband became the God.

Most traditional May Day activities center around this renewal of life, the culmination of the fertility of spring and the first day of summer's bounty. May baskets are made and filled with flowers, then left anonymously on the door of a friend, and of course what celebration would be complete without the maypole? This obvious symbol of the God's fecundity has managed to survive through the years festooned with ribbons as it always has been, and will continue to be so as long as people honor the sacredness of spring.

The ancient Romans used garlands and swags of flowers and greenery to decorate their temples and each other on Floralia, their festival to honor Flora, goddess of flowers. Naturally, Floralia occurred on or around May 1 and was adopted into the Christian calendar as May Day later on.

Many flowers are at their peak as the bees visit them, gathering their pollen and drinking their nectar. These amazing insects help plants have their own kind of sex, specifically the plants that do not have self-fertile flowers. They carry the pollen from one flower's male parts to another flower's female parts (or from a male flower to a female flower if the plant bears these instead) and we get apples or tomatoes or rose hips or walnuts or any number of other kinds of fruits.

Bees themselves, apart from the scientific observations of their complex operations, have long been held as sacred. The ancient Egyptians, Greeks, Maya, Europeans, Scandinavians, Jews, and Christians (and probably many others) all have honored bees in various ways, and honeybees in particular for their delicious honey and production of valuable multipurpose wax. Whether delivering the souls of the departed to heaven or ferrying back the nectar of immortality, the bee has also been seen as a messenger of the heavens, and some tales also center around the fact that honeybees die after stinging.

Out in the garden one evening I was watching a fuzzy yellow-and-black bumblebee visit my cosmos flowers. It was dusk and the temperature can drop quickly up here in the mountains, so the bee found itself suddenly unable to fly (bumblebees cannot fly if their body temperature falls below 86 degrees). It clung to the center of the cosmos flower all night, something like a climber hanging a sleeping bag off the side of the sheer cliff face he's ascending. In the morning the bee was up before I was, but it had simply resumed the business of visiting all the cosmos flowers when the sun came up, and I watched it clamber among the pollen-filled stamens for several minutes before it finally flew away.

I found that I enjoyed slowing down to watch the simple show just as the bee lives its life in that slow and simple way, no place it had to "bee" but there, at that moment, on that flower. Reserve some time as often as you can to just "bee." Share this time with your family or alone, travel to a place of quiet or just look at the clouds or flowers in your own backyard. On Beltane, have your guests spend a few minutes in relaxed silence with a partner, simply holding each other or looking into each other's eyes. Let the time be filled with love for each other and the world.

The Lord and Lady of the May

One ancient tradition is the crowning of the May King and Queen, sometimes called "Robin Hood and Maid Marion" in the renaissance and after or Lord and Lady of the May. They preside over the May Day festivities, such as the maypole and games. More often in later times, especially in America where the Puritans frowned on frivolities like May Day, only a May Queen was chosen, something like a Prom Queen, accompanied by a court of ladies-in-waiting. So if you have a shortage of men in your coven (like none), you can elect a Lady of the May and still keep with tradition. Obviously the reverse is true as well, and all-male covens should feel welcome to elect a Lord of the May to preside over the day.

There are many ways to choose the Lord and Lady of the May, such as hidden ballot election, drawing lots, or keeping to the old tradition of choosing "the fairest" man and woman to serve. Of course, the group's interpretation of what "fair" means is up to them. Since May Day is the last day of spring and welcomes in the summer, teens or twentysomethings are perhaps the most appropriate choice for the day's royalty. *Walford's Antiquarian*, published in 1886, gives an account from Oxfordshire, England, in 1774 of how these two temporary nobles were selected:

> In choosing the Lord and Lady of the May, care was taken to select a smart, active, and handsome man, as well as a lively, pretty woman, the daughter of some respectable farmer, and to whom it often proved the prelude of obtaining a husband. It is doubtful whether the Lord derived any pecuniary advantage

from the revenue that supported his state, though the Lady was allowed daily new shoes and twenty yards of ribbon, and, at the end of the sports, was complimented with a guinea.

However they are selected, the May King and Queen don't just sit on a dais decorated with flowers—their work includes blessing the festivities, awarding prizes to the winners of games, and getting to be first in line at the potluck buffet table. If your group is large enough and you wish to have a parade, the King and Queen walk at the head of the procession, the Lady carrying her traditional bouquet of flowers, or may even be carried on litters. If your local area still has a May Day parade and your group is "out," you could even make a floral float and have the Lord and Lady of the May atop it. Traditionally accompanying the Lord and Lady would be any attendants and a jester or harlequin figure brandishing a sand-filled leather bladder on a stick at the crowd to make them get out of the path of the royal procession.

Bell Parade

Morris dancers are famous for wearing bells to "wake up the earth," and many European May Day traditions include ringing bells for this purpose. In England, some towns hold a parade where everyone is given a bell, then all the people walk in a joyeous procession, ringing their bells to encourage new growth and prosperity.

Some say that the bells also chase away evil spirits from the area, and in the Middle Ages it became popular to also "chase away the witches" on the night of April 30 with lots of noise. In Germany, however, noise is used around the houses of childless couples to help them conceive on Beltane, so you might want to incorporate this idea into your May Day activities.

The Maypole

One of the best-known and oldest traditions of Beltane is the maypole. I have to laugh when I see books and Web sites claim that "the meaning

Folded paper animals add charm and bright color to a Yule table centerpiece.

Flint-and-steel firestarting: use charcloth to help the kindling catch fire.

Yule

Paper cornucopias like these were popular in Victorian times.

Trimming greens for decorating a kissing ball.

Imbolc

A finished skein of homespun yarn and a drop spindle; the spindle shows how to loop the yarn on top and bottom.

A new candle made from recycled chunks of burned-down-candle wax.

Ostara

A straw-bale cold frame for starting seeds for later planting.

Gathering willow branches for basket weaving.

Green willow basket: finishing the bottom.

Finishing the sides and weaving through the handle.

A completed willow basket.

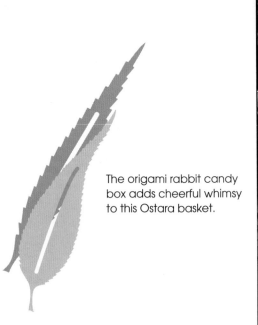

The origami rabbit candy box adds cheerful whimsy to this Ostara basket.

A sparkling spun-sugar nest.

of the maypole has long been lost." I don't know about you, but I can't think of a more obvious fertility symbol than "erecting" an enormous wooden pole, burying one end in the soil, and bedecking it with flowers and ribbons!

Here are a few lines from a maypole song of 1673 that give more of a picture of how our ancestors might have celebrated the holiday:

> *About the May-pole we dance all a-round,*
> *And with garlands of pinks and roses are crown'd;*
> *Our little kind tribute we merrily pay,*
> *To the gay Lad and bright Lady o' th' May.*

The pole should, ideally, be of naturally straight wood, such as a young sapling tree from which the branches have been stripped. You'll want to decorate and bless the pole before erecting it—some groups simply use a flower garland at the top while some make a complicated hanging wheel sort of arrangement that covers the top like a crown of flowers. As can be seen from the above poem, two of the traditional flowers used on Beltane are pinks and roses, both in full bloom on May first. Pinks today are usually known by their genus name of "dianthus," and there are many kinds of flowers in this fragrant family including tiny "sweet williams," and huge florist's carnations. If you want to be historically correct, however, you want what's known as a "clove pink" or "dianthus" in shades from white through pink to red or dark pink. The smaller florist's carnation in shades of pink and white would work too, although it's much fuller than a nonhybrid variety of true pinks. Roses, too, should be the single pink variety if you want a medieval look to your decorations, since modern hybrid tea roses did not exist in 1673. But naturally, you can decorate your maypole however you like, perhaps by having your guests bring flowers from their own gardens to share.

It's easy to make a permanent place to "plant" your maypole every year. You'll need to use the same pole or poles with the same diameter at the base. From the hardware store, get about two feet or three feet of pipe with an inner diameter that's slightly larger than the diameter of your pole—you'll need less pipe if your pole is shorter, more if it's taller.

Dig a shaft into the earth to fit your length of pipe and set it inside vertically. Backfill any extra earth around the outsides of the pipe and tamp it down very securely. When you're ready to erect the maypole, simply place the end in the pipe and use small wooden shims (also available at the hardware store) or sticks to wedge the pole tightly into the pipe. When you're all done, cover the pipe and hole with a large stepping stone for safety.

Once the pole is safely up and ready to be ribboned, gather some musicians from your group and have them sing or play a jaunty tune, or use recorded music for the people to dance to as they go around (I think "Up and About" by the Chieftains is perfect for this). You need an even number of participants. Have each one grab a ribbon, then have every other person face either right or left so that you have pairs facing each other. Then proceed to skip, dance or walk in opposite directions, each person going over and then under and then over the ribbons of the people as they come to them in turn, creating a lovely interwoven design in the ribbons as they cover the pole. You can then either leave the pole ribboned until the end of the day or leave it until next year, covering last year's ribbons with new ones. Alternately, you can have the people reverse directions and unwind the ribbons, then let them take their ribbon home for luck and love.

May Games

Beside the erecting and decorating of the maypole, the Lord and Lady of the May oversee the May games. Historic accounts of these include country dances (much like our modern square dancing without the calling) under a specially constructed arching bower covered with greenery and flowers. Another activity was the making up of "fines." The Lord and Lady would list off various situations that would incur a penalty or monetary fine, such as kissing, burping, eating corn chips, petting the cat . . . whatever your royalty decrees. The miscreant then refuses to pay the fine on purpose or otherwise is subjected to the penalty at hand.

You can get creative as to what the "penalty" should be, depending on the group. One traditional "penalty" is given in *Walford's Antiquarian*:

> . . . He that refused to pay was forced to ride my Lord's horse. This was a wooden machine, about four feet high, borne upon poles, and having the head of a horse with a bridle. Upon this my Lady first mounted, sideways, holding the rein; then the delinquent was placed behind her, and both carried by two men around the May-pole. . . . During the ride it became the duty of the swain to salute my Lady; and whether he was a bashful or gay gallant, the process always proved a subject of merriment for the spectators.

Other ideas for May games are traditional medieval and renaissance games, like using padded quarterstaffs to try to knock an opponent off a log, and "cloches," where one ball is the target and participants try to toss or roll their balls as close to the target as possible (almost exactly like lawn bowls). Naturally, more modern games are also great fun at a Beltane celebration, and our women's coven brought a unique penis ring toss game to the regional Pagan festivities by way of a phallus-shaped candle and some cardboard rings. Other ideas you might like to try include a "bran box" which is a box of sand with prizes hidden inside, a game of horseshoes, a fund-raising coin-toss board (paint a piece of plywood in brightly-colored sections and players try to toss coins into them to win prizes) and so on. Bawdy or not, it's easy to devise some simple games that are fun for a crowd. The Lord and Lady of the May award prizes to the winners of the games, such as sweets or flowers.

Another traditional activity, one that isn't really a game, is the battle between winter and summer. Two groups of young men would face off, one in winter clothing and one in summer clothing, and fight a mock battle with the summer group always winning. The victors would then parade around the maypole singing that "we have brought the summer home" while carrying green branches and flowers. Naturally, your Lord and Lady of the May could award these flowers to the winning side as part of your festivities.

May Baskets

One May Day tradition that has only just recently petered out here in the U.S. is the leaving of anonymous may baskets. Schoolchildren would make them and leave them on the doorknob or doorstep of people they liked, ring the bell, and then run away to hide and watch the recipient's reaction from the secrecy of nearby shrubbery. Most often these baskets would be little paper baskets with handles filled with just-picked garden flowers, wildflowers, or sometimes little gifts like penny candy. May baskets would be a fun party favor for your guests to receive or even to make themselves. Have some pretty papers on hand and make simple cones with handles (see page 15 for paper cone ideas) or provide miniature wicker baskets purchased at the craft store. You can also make your own fresh baskets out of willow branches or other green sticks (see page 69 for basket making instructions). The leaving of may baskets is such a lovely spring tradition that shows your affection for others—keep it alive by sharing it with everyone you know and love.

Magic Dew

As on Midsummer, the morning dew found on May Day appears to have magical properties, according to tradition. Both in Europe and in parts of America, women wash their faces in May dew to preserve a youthful visage, improve the complexion, and enhance their beauty. Some of the traditions surrounding the gathering and use of May dew can be quite complicated! One method, used to cure illness, requires the gatherer to collect the dew from the grave of the most recently buried person of the opposite sex after waving their hands up and down the grave three times. Another tradition is to roll naked in the dew so that "even the plainest girl will be given great beauty." May dew is also used to cure just about everything, including skin problems, assorted foot problems, weak backs, sore throats, freckles, sunburns, wrinkles, headaches, and sore eyes. It's also supposed to bestow luck upon the user. According to the Irish, another peculiar gift of May dew is that of knot wrangling—anyone washing their hands in it would be given the ability to undo any tangled threads or ropes easily, mend nets, and open locks.

Some locations are popular traditional spots for gathering May dew, such as Arthur's Seat in Edinburgh, Scotland, and even some types of plants are preferred over others, with green wheatgrass garnering the most favor and herb plants being next most efficacious. According to a text of 1652, the dew was gathered before sunrise with clean linen cloths and wrung out into basins for use. Some was bottled for future use and kept on a sunny windowsill or in with the medicinal herbs, much like we keep rubbing alcohol or hydrogen peroxide in any basic first aid kit. The dew was periodically poured out of the bottle and into another one, leaving behind any impurities, and was kept for medicinal purposes until the next May Day.

If you have a group over the night before Beltane, make sure they stay until dawn so you can all go outside and gather May dew. Provide small linen cloths and bowls, and have people pair off with one dragging the cloth over the grass and the other holding the bowl so that it doesn't spill. Also give everyone a small glass bottle for their dew and use a little funnel to pour it into the bottles. Let everyone combine their bowls together, or have each person collect their own with their individual energies.

For the Birds

Beltane is also the time for birds to build their nests, mate, and produce young. You and your guests can help out our feathered friends (or "winged ones" as the Native Americans call them) in a lot of ways. First, determine what birds you have in your area and what their needs are. Some birds like birdhouses and nest boxes, but they don't all use the same size house or entry hole, so you'll need to find out what they like best. Some birds make their own nests and might like some yarn and dryer lint put out for their building efforts. Use brightly colored yarns so you can more easily spot the nests you helped them make. Cut off 6- to

12-inch lengths of yarn and hang them from trees or leave them on the ground where you've seen birds gathering grasses and twigs.

Bird feeders should be cleaned and filled with fresh food as well. Once again, determine what kinds of birds you have and what kinds of foods they like. Some prefer ordinary grocery store seed, while some will only show up for things like thistle seed, nectar, suet, peanuts, sliced citrus fruit, raisins, or insects. Any kind of native plants that promote birds should be planted now as well, especially those that produce nectar and attract both hummingbirds and butterflies. Get your coven-mates involved by having them make simple bird feeders and bird houses from kits, giving them bird-friendly plants as gifts, or simply going out on a group birdwatching walk together on May Day.

A Blessing and a Feast

A Scottish tradition from the highlands is to create a brew of eggs, butter, oatmeal, and milk in a large pot. After cooking, some of the pot is then spilled on the ground as a libation, along with alcohol and whatever people have brought for the occasion. A specially baked oatcake is then broken apart and shared, pieces being flung over the shoulder to ask for blessings on various crops and animals as well as to try to appease various problem animals like foxes and crows. After the oatcake is gone, the feast begins in earnest, and the oatmeal dish in the pot is a part of the banquet.

CRAFTS

Beltane Stitchery

The birds, the bees, and the flowers are all doing it this time of year. This verdant green field adds vibrancy to a deep red rose ready to give to a lover (after the bee's done with it). (For additional stitchery instructions and suggestions, see pages 211–214.)

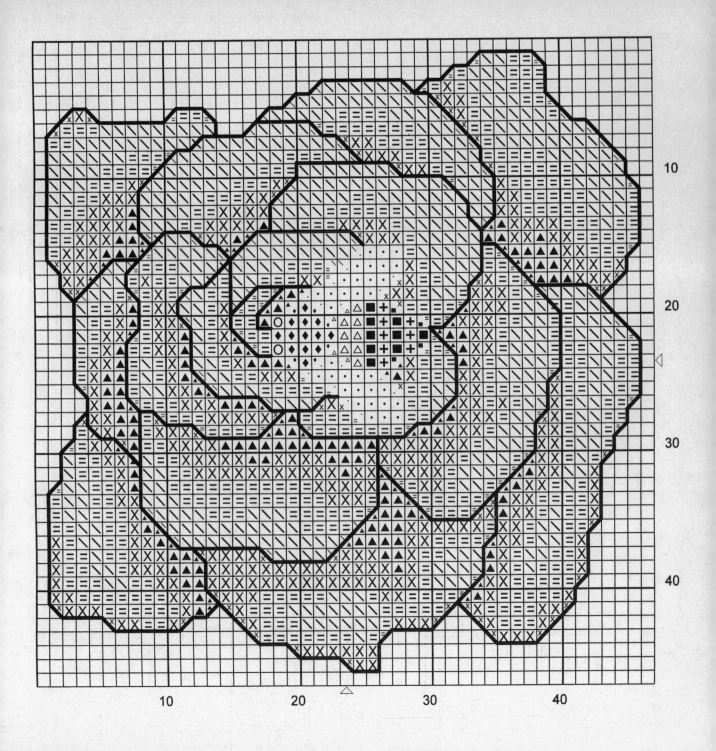

Grid Size: 47 W × 47 H
Cloth Count: 18
Fabric: Green Aida
Design Area: 2.61″ W × 2.61″ H (45 × 45 stitches)

Pattern Key

Symbol	DMC Floss		Color
■	310	(2 strands)	Black
+	3820	(2 strands)	Straw—dark
♦	612	(2 strands)	Drab brown—light
△	3822	(2 strands)	Straw—light
=	321	(2 strands)	Christmas red
X	498	(2 strands)	Christmas red—dark
\	3801	(2 strands)	Christmas red—light
▲	814	(2 strands)	Garnet—dark
·	White	(2 strands)	White
	Mill Hill		
O	Seed bead		black

Backstitches

Symbol	DMC Floss		Color
——	814	(1 strand)	Garnet—dark

Note: Use of Mill Hill seed beads for the eyes is optional. If desired, stitch squares with black floss only. For bee backstitching, see the following chart.

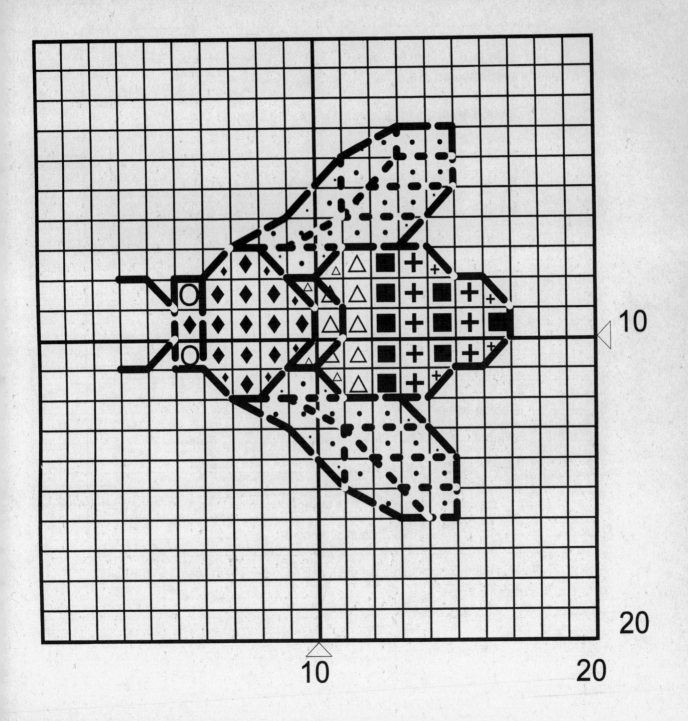

10

20

10

20

Grid Size:	20 W × 20 H	
Cloth Count:	18	
Fabric:	Aida	
Design Area:	1.11″ W × 1.11″ H (14 × 13 stitches)	

Pattern Key

Symbol	DMC Floss (2 strands)	Color
■	310	Black
·	White	White
♦	612	Drab brown
△	3822	Straw—light
+	3820	Straw—dark
	Mill Hill	
O	Seed bead	Black

Backstitches

Symbol	DMC Floss (1 strand)	Color
——	310	Black
	Kreinik (1 strand)	
- - -	105C antique silver cord	

Note: Add the two black beads for eyes last, so threads won't catch on the beads while you are stitching.

Love Cards

Who says you can only send romantic cards on the Christian St. Valentine's Day? Beltane is our holiday to be with loved ones and lovers, so show them how you really feel with handmade cards you put yourself into.

YOU'LL NEED:

Blank notecards with envelopes (optional)

Scrapbooking paper in various colors

Markers in various colors

Rubber stamps, ink, and accessories

Satin ribbons in various colors

Paper lace doilies

Pressed flowers

Stickers

Embossed Victorian paper decoupage cutouts

If not using blank notecards, cut the scrapbooking paper to the size you want and fold it in half, white side in. Pick whatever methods of designing the card you like best and let your imagination run wild! Some ideas to get you started are:

Maypole: Cut a piece of tan construction paper in the shape of a pole and lay it down where you want it. Mark under the top of the pole and glue the ends of several different colored ribbons on the mark. Glue down the pole and then attach a few more ribbons on top of the pole. Hide the rough edges of the ribbons with a pressed or paper flower and add paper grass at the bottom.

Victorian romance: Cut a heart from a round lace doily (or use a heart-shaped doily if you can find one) and use this for the body of the card. Attach embossed paper cutouts, pressed flowers, ribbons, stickers, and so on to create a typically over-the-top Victorian message of love. Many Victorian designs can be found that feature a lady's hand or a bird with a little message of love written on a scroll.

Great Rite: Make copies of your favorite erotica or clip pictures out of an adult toy catalog to make a unique card for that special someone. Alternately, you could show the chalice-and-blade imagery on the front of the card and write something appropriate inside.

Rose Petal Beads

The origins of this ancient craft stretch back to perhaps ancient Greece, and it appears that the devotional strand of "rosary" beads were so named because they were first created with rose petal beads like these. There are many variations on how to make these beads, which usually turn out wine colored, dark brown, or black, depending on whether you use a stainless steel, enamel, or old iron pot (the latter turns them black). Use the fragrant beads as Beltane gifts and in ritual jewelry.

YOU'LL NEED:

4 cups fresh red rose petals
Food processor or blender
2-quart saucepan (see types above)
¼ cup sliced citrus peel (optional)
½ teaspoon cinnamon or other spices (optional)
1 tablespoon ground dried orris root powder
Several drops rose oil
Straight pins
Cardboard

Make sure your rose petals are completely organic and have not been sprayed with anything. Being by picking off the hard bottoms of the petals and discarding them. Put the rose petals in the blender, add a little water (1 or 2 tablespoons), and purée into a pulp. Pour this pulp into a lidded pot, adding a little more water if needed, cover, and simmer the mixture for several hours to break down the heavy structure of the petals. Add citrus peels and/or spices while simmering if desired.

Pour the petal mixture through a very fine strainer, cheesecloth, or jelly bag. Pick out any citrus peel you may have added and press the pulp to remove any excess water, reserving the liquid for other craft projects. Thoroughly and completely mix in the orris powder and rose oil. You should now have a rose petal "dough" that can be shaped into beads. If the pulp will not stick together or form beads, press out more liquid or allow the mixture to sit for a couple of hours in a warm place.

Form beads by firmly pressing blobs of pulp together and then rolling balls of the pulp between your hands, making them about twice as large as you want the finished beads to be to allow for shrinkage. While still wet, skewer each finished bead onto a straight pin and push the pin into a piece of cardboard for drying. Place the cardboard in a gas oven with just the pilot light, or set it in a sunny window to help the beads dry faster and prevent molding. Every few hours, gently twist the bead on the pin so that it won't dry onto it and be impossible to remove later. After a few days, the beads will be completely dry and you can slide them off the pins. Store your finished beads or jewelry made from them in a dry location that can breathe, such as your linen cabinet or altar. Do not store these beads in plastic bags or they may mildew. When the beads begin to lose their fragrance in time (this can be months or years), rub them with rose oil to revitalize the scent.

Living Wreaths

This variation on the traditional topiary can be made in a number of ways and with many types of plants. I've selected a number of different pretty and drought-tolerant flowers and plants for this wreath so you get a lovely display with less fuss and lower watering requirements. After a few weeks, it's best to place the plants out in your garden so they can continue to grow and flourish all summer (and beyond for the perennial varieties).

YOU'LL NEED:

About 2 pounds sphagnum moss
24-inch wire wreath form
1 pound potting soil
1 six-pack 'Snow Crystals' alyssum
1 six-pack mixed color alyssum (pinks, purples, roses, etc.)
1 six-pack variegated thyme (like 'Lime' or 'Argenteus')
1 six-pack lamb's ears (*Stachys byzantina*)
1 six-pack assorted trailing verbenas
1 six-pack fleabane (*Erigeron*)
1 package straight hairpins or topiary clips

Wet the moss by soaking it in a bucket before you start. When it's saturated, lay the wire form on your patio or a newspaper-covered table and start filling the form with the moss, packing it in generously until the form is full. Make a little trench in the middle of the moss and fill it with potting soil. Find where the top hanger of the wire wreath is and place that side away from you.

Begin planting the wreath plants by nestling the roots down into the potting soil and pressing them in firmly, tipping them this way and that to give a natural look.. Keep mixing the assorted plants randomly and pleasingly until you're out of room in the wreath. Tuck more moss in where needed to hide any exposed soil. Stand the wreath up as it will hang and pin down any trailing plants to the moss with the topiary clips.

Check for moistness every day by sticking your finger down into the soil and water the wreath as needed (probably every day if the weather is hot or every other day if it's been cool) by soaking it for a few minutes in a large basin or tub until any bubbles stop coming out. Allow to hang until it stops dripping and replace on your door or outdoor wall.

Flower and Greenery Leis

In Hawaii, May Day is known as "Lei Day." It's easy to see why—the traditional flower-and-greenery lei is just as appropriate to Beltane festivities as the European and American flower-filled baskets and garlands. You can make a haku lei for your head, the more familiar necklace lei, or smaller leis for around your wrists and ankles if you leave enough string on each end to tie them on.

YOU'LL NEED:

Embroidery floss (any color)
Large embroidery or upholstery needle
Light, fragrant flowers like jasmine, plumeria, miniature roses, gardenia,
    tuberose, miniature carnations, small orchids, etc.
Greenery like small fern fronds, small citrus leaves, ti leaves, ginger
    leaves, etc.
Small shells or colorful feathers (optional)

Thread a 36-inch length of floss onto the needle, knotting one end. As you work, pierce the flowers either through the center or horizontally with the needle and slide them down the thread to the knot. Mix in the greenery, piercing the fronds or citrus leaves and allowing them to stick out from the flowers and form a lovely contrast. Long leaves like the ti or ginger should be woven onto the needle by stitching through them several times down their length and then be drawn into a ruffle as you slide it to the bottom of the floss. You can also add shells and colorful feathers which are also traditional materials (but not ordinarily mixed with fresh floral materials). Check the length of your lei by pinching the ends of the thread together and tie it off in a square knot when you're done. Use them the same day if possible or refrigerate overnight.

Scented Massage Oils

Yeah baby! I am a massage fiend, and anyone who misses the opportunity for a fragrant oil massage on Beltane has her priorities backwards. If you're making this oil to surprise your lover, make sure you know what his or her favorite fragrance is and try to make one using that scent.

YOU'LL NEED:

Small funnel
2 ounces almond, extra virgin olive, or other neutral cosmetic oil
3 ounces flip-top or pump bottle
20–40 drops essential oils of your choice
Decorative labels
Fine-tip permanent marker

Use the funnel to help pour the cosmetic base oil into the bottle. Add the essential oils, put the lid on the bottle, and shake vigorously to mix. Label your massage oil and you're done!

Mix and match the oils as desired, using your personal preferences or established aromatherapy guidelines. Romantic mixtures could include rose, gardenia, jasmine, and ylang-ylang. Relaxing oils could feature lavender, chamomile, and cedar. For an energizing massage, try citrus, sandalwood, and eucalyptus.

MENU

Steamed Asparagus Tips

Heart-Shaped Bruschetta

Edible Flower Salad With Fiddleheads

Strawberry Topiary With Dips

Amazingly Rich Chocolate Tofu Cheesecake

Sparkling Fruit Juices, Shirley Temples With Cherries

Steamed Asparagus Tips

Did someone say the Green Man is here? As the server, you get to decide where the dressing is drizzled, so get playful.

2 pounds asparagus spears, pencil thickness

FOR THE DRESSING

2 egg yolks	1/4 teaspoon salt
1 tablespoon sugar	2 cups vegetable oil
1 tablespoon lemon juice	1/2 cup sour cream or plain yogurt

To make the dressing, combine the egg yolks, sugar, lemon juice, and salt in a medium bowl with an electric mixer. Add the vegetable oil a little at a time in a very thin, continuous stream until it has all been added and the dressing appears opaque and thickened. Whip in the sour cream or yogurt until blended and store in the refrigerator until ready to use. This dressing will keep for up to a week.

Wash the asparagus spears, then cut them in half and discard the thick butt ends. Steam until just tender and still bright green, remove from heat and rinse immediately in cold water to stop the cooking action. Drain the spears, then arrange them on a platter or on individual plates, drizzle with dressing, and serve hot. The dressing can also be spooned into a condiment squeeze bottle and used to decorate the plate or squirted artistically over the asparagus. 3–4 servings.

Heart-Shaped Bruschetta

Beltane is really our "Valentine's Day," and you'll have fun making (and eating) these red, crispy, succulent Italian toasts for two or for a crowd.

6 slices sourdough French bread (1 inch thick)	2 tablespoons red, orange, or yellow bell pepper, minced
Olive oil	2 tablespoons sun dried tomatoes, minced
1¼ cups chopped tomatoes (Roma or vine-ripened)	1 tablespoon garlic, minced
½ cup chopped marinated artichoke hearts	1 tablespoon fresh oregano, minced
¼ cup fresh basil, minced	1 tablespoon fresh Italian parsley, minced
¼ cup olive oil	Salt and black pepper to taste
3 or 4 calamata olives, pitted and minced	Grated Asiago cheese or three-cheese blend

Cut the bread slices into heart shapes using either a very sharp cookie cutter or a knife. Brush one side with olive oil and toast on a cookie sheet for one minute in the broiler, then brush the other side and toast the same way. Set aside.

In a medium bowl, combine all other ingredients except the cheese. This mixture can be chilled and served cold atop the crispy toasted bread, or the dish can be served hot—spread the tomato mixture over the bread, sprinkle it lightly with the cheese, and place the bruchettas in the broiler for a few minutes or until the cheese just begins to melt. 3–6 servings.

Edible Flower Salad With Fiddleheads

This unique salad really is the height of romance. And the complex flavors, from peppery to sweet, will delight and surprise you as the meal "unfurls." Make sure all flowers are positively identified and are free of chemical sprays before putting them before your loved ones. Use a light oil-and-vinegar dressing to enhance the salad without overpowering the delicacy of the flavors.

2	cups mixed baby greens	1/3	cup mixed herb flowers, such as chives, mint, oregano, thyme, etc.
1	cup red rose petals		
1	cup nasturtium petals		
1/2	cup pansy petals	1/3	cup radish flowers
1/2	cup daylily petals, torn into bite-size pieces	1/4	cup lavender flowers
		1/4	cup violet petals, fresh or candied (optional)
1/2	cup squash-blossom petals, torn into bite-size pieces	1 1/2	cups cooked fiddleheads

Wash and spin or pat dry all greens and flowers. Lay the mixed greens in the bottom of a large salad bowl. Sprinkle the rose, nasturtium, pansy, daylily, and squash petals on top. Toss together the herb, radish, and lavender flowers, sprinkle on top of salad. Garnish with violet petals, placing them in a neat cluster in the center of the salad mound. Place the fiddleheads around the edges of the bowl, arranging them attractively on top of the flower petals. Drizzle with dressing. 6–8 servings.

Strawberry Topiary With Dips

Have you ever been to one of those fancy parties where watermelons are carved into swans and fanciful pigs are sculpted out of lunchmeat? Ever wonder why it is nobody gets to eat all that cool-looking garnish food? Well now you can—and your guests will love you for it.

1 small clay or ceramic flowerpot
Handful of gravel, marbles, stones, etc.
About 1/2 pound modeling clay
1 foam cone 1/2 inch smaller than the diameter of the pot
Dark green acrylic craft paint
1/2-inch flat brush
1/2-inch dowel cut to 10 inches long

5-inch foam ball
Utility knife
1 small package floral moss
2 1/2 to 3 pounds fresh strawberries, selected for uniform size and appearance
1 box round toothpicks
1 yard 1/2-inch-wide ribbon any color you like
Assorted dips (see p. 105)

If your flowerpot has been used previously, scrub well and let dry. Place the gravel in the bottom of the pot to a depth of about an inch (this adds weight to the base so the topiary won't be too top heavy). Make the clay into a thick rope and line the insides of the pot (this will help hold the foam in place and add more weight). Cut the foam cone so that when placed inside the pot it comes just up to the top. Narrow end down, push the foam into place, using a knife or other tool to push the clay so that it holds the foam securely all the way around the pot.

Cut the dowel to length and paint it dark green. You can also paint the foam ball at this point if you don't want to leave it plain white, or even cover it with fabric. When the dowel is dry, use the utility knife to shave down both ends into points, so that they look something like a sharpened pencil. Push the dowel into the foam as far as it will go, making sure it is absolutely vertical. Now push the foam ball onto the other end of the dowel so that it is held very securely. Don't let the dowel tip push through the top of the ball. Tuck the moss around the foam in the flowerpot, pushing it firmly around all the edges so that it helps hold everything in place securely. Press more moss over the foam as needed to hide it and finish by pressing the moss into a nice dome shape.

Wash the strawberries and place them on a large plate so you can select from them more easily. Starting at the top of the ball, push a toothpick halfway in to the foam. Skewer a strawberry onto the pick, then start placing picks and strawberries around this first berry one at a time. Continue covering the foam ball with picks and berries, fitting them as close together as possible. When you get near the bottom of the ball, push the toothpicks in at a more horizontal angle so that the berries won't want to slide off the picks. Use two picks at slightly different angles to help hold them even better.

When all the berries are in place, start at the bottom of the dowel and crisscross a length of ribbon up to the bottom of the strawberries. Tie the ribbon in a bow and trim the ends to the desired length. The topiary will be surprisingly heavy (about 4 to 5 pounds), so carry it carefully with both hands and avoid moving it when possible.

Suggested dips: Hot caramel, hot fudge, chocolate syrup, honey, brown sugar, whipped cream, yogurt, rose water, sour cream, honey whipped with butter and cinnamon . . . let your imagination run wild!

Amazingly Rich Chocolate Tofu "Cheesecake"

I know what you're thinking. "Tofu? Are you nuts?" Trust me—this is guiltless ultra-chocolate decadence, almost as good as sex, especially when you use a premade "reduced fat" graham cracker pie crust rather than the buttery version below.

FOR THE CRUST

1½ cups graham cracker crumbs
¼ cup walnuts, very finely minced
¼ cup pecans, very finely minced
⅓ cup butter, softened

FOR THE FILLING

3 12.3-ounce packages firm "lite" tofu, drained and room temperature
3 cups sugar
1 tablespoon lemon juice
2 teaspoons vanilla extract
½ teaspoon cinnamon
¼ teaspoon salt
5 squares unsweetened chocolate

GARNISH

Whipped cream
2 large strawberries, sliced
Ghirardelli Double Chocolate hot cocoa mix

Preheat the oven to 350 degrees F. To make the crust, combine all crust ingredients and press into the bottom and sides of an 8- or 9-inch springform cake pan (you can use any straight-sided cake pan if you will be serving it from the pan and not unmolding the cake for presentation). Bake for five minutes and set aside.

Purée the tofu, one package at a time, until absolutely smooth with no lumps remaining. Pour into a large mixing bowl. Whisk in the sugar, lemon juice, vanilla, cinnamon, and salt. Cut the chocolate squares in half. Melt the chocolate in a double boiler or place in a glass measuring cup and melt it in the microwave for about 2 minutes at 60 percent power. The chocolate should be very liquid with no lumps. Quickly whisk the melted chocolate into the tofu mixture until completely blended. Pour into the graham cracker crust, using custard cups to cook any excess filling. Bake for about 40 minutes, 25 minutes for custard cups. Remove from oven and chill completely before serving. Atop each slice, place a dollop of whipped cream, a slice of strawberry, and dust lightly with cocoa mix. Serves about 10 lovers.

DECORATIONS

Flowers: Nothing says May or romance like flowers. Garlands of flowers should be draped everywhere, wreaths of flowers should be hung on every door and over the altar, overflowing baskets and vases filled with fresh floral bouquets should be placed wherever there's a spot of room, and flowering plants in pots should be tucked into corners, given as gifts, or placed in sunny windows. And think of the possibilities for artificial flowers! Use silk flowers wherever you would use real flowers but need longevity because of wear or ritual use, such as attaching them to maypole streamers, creating permanent ritual altar pieces, or making seasonal wreaths to last a lifetime. Even floral look-alikes or items with flowers on them, like strings of covered mini lights, flower-print dishes, candles, and floral paperware work perfectly for Beltane. There is literally no end to the decorating uses for flowers, whether real or simulated.

Roses: The rose is the quintessential flower of romance. There are whole codes of the meanings of rose colors, and these can vary, but usually red roses mean true love and passion, pink roses stand for affection, white roses connotate purity and innocence, and yellow roses can be either friendship or remembrance. A simple vase of cut rose stems is a lovely accent for the altar or the nightstand. Use them everywhere on Beltane, and don't forget to use items that look like roses or have roses on them in romantic ways too.

Strewn flower petals: If you have an abundance of roses or any other large-petaled flower in your garden, it's marvelously romantic to scatter the petals all over the ground, the thrones for the Lord and Lady of the May, the banquet tables, a procession walkway (perhaps by a flower girl?) and, of course, furniture and beds.

Maypole: Naturally, this part of traditional Beltane activities is highly decorative in itself. But if you can't have a maypole or it's not part of your ritual, use tiny ones made from dowels and other craft supplies, or purchase small "lollipop" topiaries and festoon them with colorful ribbons.

Ribbons: If you just want to give an impressionistic feeling of a maypole, use many colors of ribbons when decorating your ritual space and home. Make curtains of ribbons and hang them over doorways so people must pass through them, tie little ribbons onto placecards and favors, braid great handfuls of ribbons into large swags for over doors and windows, and use ribbons all over your hair and body too.

Lace: Whether white or colored, lace can represent the Maiden's innocence, the frivolity of spring, or the sensuality of lingerie. Just as you would use ribbons, use strands of lace as streamers and garlands, serve food in dishes printed with a lace pattern, or have all your guests wear something with lace on it just for fun. Give them little party favors of round lace doilies filled with rose potpourri and tied shut with a colorful ribbon.

Images of sexual deities, Sheila-Na-Gig, Pan, satyrs, Herne, Shiva/Shakti

5

LITHA/SUMMER SOLSTICE/MIDSUMMER

(June 20–23)

Bittersweet in its celebration, the summer solstice is the apex of the sun's strength but also the moment he begins his descent into death. The duality of the Oak and Holly kings is honored now as at Yule, with the Holly King of the waning year wresting rule from the Oak King of spring's new life. The decline of the year is acknowledged, but not truly recognized as yet since there's a lot of good weather still to be had and bountiful harvests to come.

The hottest weather has not yet begun, the heat of August around the corner yet. And it is this blistering heat that kills—the power of the waning king causes crops to both wither and ripen—without the ripening death of the golden grains, we would not have the bread that sustains us.

Like many of our sabbats, Midsummer is considered to be one of the times when the veil is thinner, and faeries come amongst the mortals. One of Shakespeare's most popular plays, *A Midsummer Night's Dream*, is based on the meddling of the Faerie Kingdom in the love lives of several mortals, with much confusion, magic, and marriage the result. Of course, June is the most popular month of the year for weddings as well.

Another traditionally important aspect of Midsummer is ritual bathing and purification. Some traditions instruct us to bathe in the light of the Midsummer sun, but others say that people would go down to the lakes and rivers to purify themselves and be endowed with health and strength. Just as on Beltane morning, ladies are also advised to wash their faces with Midsummer dew "so they will be lovely throughout the year."

Flowers are another important aspect of Midsummer, especially the roses which are at their height of beauty. In Scandinavia, Midsummer festivities are a lot like Beltane farther south (presumably because of the climate) and include romance, flower divination to find your future mate, and even a maypole. In Cornwall, England, a Midsummer ceremony that is traditionally performed in Cornish centers around the tossing of a mixed bouquet of flowers and weeds into the bonfire. The "Lady of the Flowers" approaches the fire and says, "In one bunch together bound, flowers for burning here are found, both good and ill. Thousandfold let good seed spring, wicked weeds, fast withering, let this fire kill!"

A traditional Midsummer song from Cornwall, which almost seems like a Beltane ballad, speaks of the solstice bonfire and quite a lot of romantic activities. Unfortunately, I've been unable to locate a source for the tune, but you could read it as a poem or do what they did in medieval times—make up your own melody.

> *The bonny month of June is crowned*
> *With the sweet scarlet rose;*
> *The groves and meadows all around*
> *With lovely pleasure flows.*

As I walked out to yonder green,
One evening so fair;
All where the fair maids may be seen
Playing at the bonfire.

Hail! lovely nymphs, be not too coy,
But freely yield your charms;
Let love inspire with mirth and joy,
In Cupid's lovely arms.

Bright Luna spreads its light around,
The gallants for to cheer;
As they lay sporting on the ground,
At the fair June bonfire.

All on the pleasant dewy mead,
They shared each other's charms;
Till Phoebus' beams began to spread,
And coming day alarms.

Whilst larks and linnets sing so sweet,
To cheer each lovely swain;
Let each prove true unto their love,
And so farewell the plain.

Midsummer is also known as St. John's Eve, and it's interesting to note that just as Jesus was born at Yule, John the Baptist was born at Litha, the duality of the kings of life and death seen once again. To further the comparison, John the Baptist is sometimes called the "Oak King" and depicted with horns and cloven feet, rather like Pan. He is also called by Jesus "a bright and shining light." English holly is sometimes called "Christ's thorn," and so we see the Holly King and Oak King wearing Christian masks. St. John's Wort is one of the traditional Midsummer decorations, and it is burned in the solstice fire with the other flowers.

Whether it be coincidence or no, St. John's Wort has a number of connections to the sun. The flowers are a lovely bright yellow, with many stamens in the center that remind one of the rays of the sun coming out from the middle of the five flat, shiny yellow petals that surround them. The attractive herb is now known to benefit those suffering from depression and SAD, or Seasonal Affective Disorder, which is thought to be aggravated by the lack of sunlight in winter. Is it any wonder that such a solar plant would be able to help bring a little summer happiness into the hearts of people that are (literally) sick of winter? But Witches don't need scientists or drug companies to tell us that.

Playing With Fire

From a purely scientific standpoint, it might seem superstitious to have a bonfire on the solstice in imitation of the sun, but science actually supports the practice in ways our ancestors couldn't have known. By burning wood and other plant materials, we are releasing the stored energy in those items. Where did the energy come from? Primarily from the sun—so by having a bonfire we truly do have a bit of the sun's fire and energy right here before us on earth.

Many groups hold a traditional Midsummer bonfire as their way of saying goodbye to the sun, mimicking its fiery nature, purifying themselves and their belongings, and getting rid of unwanted things. Some bonfire customs called for two smaller fires which people walked and drove their livestock between to ensure good health, while others had one large fire that people walked around deosil for the same purpose.

So maybe you're not the fiery type or are a city person who has never even had a fireplace let alone built a bonfire. That's okay, it's not that hard. Assuming you have a place to build a giant bonfire and have obtained the proper permits, start by clearing a circle about five or six feet across of all debris. Surround the edges with large stones, bricks, an earthen berm, or other nonburnable edging material. Make sure you remove all large rocks from the fire pit since some rocks contain traces of moisture inside them and will explode when subjected to intense heat. Gather up LOTS of very dry bonfire materials—this can be anything from old wooden furniture to the brush you cut out of the side yard a month ago and never got out to the curb (make sure you do not burn poison oak or poison ivy as the inhaled smoke can be deadly!!). Ideally, you'll want something smaller to get the fire started in the middle, one-inch diameter kindling, and various lengths of branches, etc., for the main fire.

To lay the fire, place a few larger branches in a criss-cross shape in the center of your prepared circle (a pentagram might be a nice choice). Lay your starter materials (candle nubs, pine needles, paper goods, etc.) in the middle of that, and make a loose "tipi" of twigs and thicker kindling over the top of the starter stuff. Make sure you leave a path to at least one candle nub or good bunch of paper so you can light the fire easily and with as little smoke as possible. Keep building up your cone of sticks, putting larger and larger wood in layers toward the outside. Remember to reserve some large pieces of firewood for later if you'll be having the bonfire for more than about a half hour. Also be sure not to make your layers of wood too tightly laid—air flow is just as important to the fire's survival as dry wood is. When you're all ready to go, have everyone stand back and light your starter material. Ideally, it should blaze up quickly and produce almost no smoke after a couple of minutes.

If you can't have an open fire in your location for whatever reason, use a candle circle instead. This can be arranged so that people can walk through a break in the circle and be purified, blessed, and healed and is especially effective for rituals held in halls in the evening. Outside, use a circle of tiki torches in the same way. In both cases, however, remind people about fire safety and inform those that like to come in elaborate robes (you know who they are) that there will be many open flames. You can try to steer these folks toward wearing something less billowy if you think they'll take your advice, otherwise have a fire extinguisher and/or bucket of sand handy (and perhaps some liability release forms if they're also clumsy).

Carrying lit torches around their fields on Midsummer was another common way for people to bless the land and the crops. You can do the same thing with candles, tiki torches, or sparklers, whether you want to bless a bit of land or each other. If you live in an area that has legal fireworks for sale, another way to liven up your Midsummer celebration is with a colorful fireworks display. Of course, if you can find any, you must include spinning firework wheels (sometimes called Catherine wheels) nailed up to a post so that they spin the direction you want.

Traditionally, in parts of northern Europe, wagon wheels covered with pitch were set afire and then rolled down a steep hillside to imitate the descent of the sun at Midsummer. Even if you can't send a tar-coated flaming wheel across the lawn this solstice, if you're having a large gathering you might like to hire a fire juggler or fire eater for the occasion. You could work him or her into the ritual if they're up for it. Of course, if you can convince one of your members to take up the hobby, the possibilities are endless!

Sword Dancing

Another summertime tradition, one with no real fixed calendar date, is the variation of morris dancing known as sword dancing. While the origins of the ritual is supposedly lost to antiquity, some of the elements seem perfect for the death of the Oak King and rise to power of the Holly King. The dancers, between five and eight usually, work with specially made blunt, supple swords. They begin with simple routines, such as a straight line that breaks to a circle like other morris dances, but as time goes on the dancing becomes more and more intricate and intense, finally ending in a "lock" of interwoven swords that can be held aloft with one hand.

There are other characters common to mummer's plays who accompany the troupe, as well as musicians or a single piper. The King character sometimes has the lock of swords dropped over his head so that his neck is surrounded by the blades, a ceremonial imitation of decapitation. The King is then resurrected by the Doctor character. If you can find a morris troupe who performs this dance or can have a group of seven people learn it, it would make a very effective climax to your midsummer ritual!

Hail, Spirits of the Southern Barbecue

At a recent midsummer ritual I organized, we called the quarters with fun versions of the usual elements—east was represented by bubbles floating on the air, the west priestess jumped into the swimming pool (which happened to be in that corner of the yard we were using), and north was called in with a bouquet of sunflowers. In the south, the priestess held aloft a tiki torch while calling the element, then touched it to a prepared barbecue pit which had been placed in the south, sort of Olympic torch style. The coals were perfect, by the end of the ritual, for the hungry crowd to barbecue whatever meats they liked right there on our south fire. Even if you can't incorporate this element into your own ritual, a barbecue is not only great summer fun, it's yet another way to bring fire into your Litha celebration.

Swim Party

If you happen to have a pool in your yard, it's a great excuse to have a midsummer pool party. Make it an annual tradition! Unless the weather is intolerable, the last half of June is a great time to go swimming and brings an extra element of fun to your gathering. Ask your guests to bring their own towels and sunscreen, however, since you don't need the hassle and mess of having to wash all those towels. You could ask each guest to bring their favorite CD that really screams "summertime" and play the music by the pool. Serve simple fingerfoods at poolside that won't crumble, get into the filter or otherwise make a mess—try stuffed celery pieces, olives, fruit slices, and cheese cubes, avoiding things like tortilla chips, crackers, and open-faced sandwiches.

If you have a lighted pool or hot tub, your party could go well into the night. Perhaps you could plan it to end at exactly sunset, with everyone giving a final farewell to the Sun King as he passes below the horizon. That's the signal—everyone out of the pool! Or, in the case of the hot tub, everyone in!

Origami Boat Races

One of the most popular events in China is the Dragon Boat Race, which commemorates the drowning of an ancient hero in the Mi Lo river. It always occurs on the fifth day of the fifth lunar month, usually around the beginning of June, and is a huge national spectacle.

Every sabbat, member covens of South Bay Circles take turns hosting the holiday, and one summer solstice we had a Chinese-themed ritual. One of the coveners of the group running that ritual is originally from China, and they did a Dragon Dance, cast the circle with traditional Chinese directions and elements, and hosted a dragon boat race in miniature across the swimming pool.

We were each given an origami boat made from heavy paper stock (instructions for making them appear later in this chapter) and materials to decorate them. Since it was a dragon boat race, I drew a dragon on mine with a gold pen and put brilliant hologram stickers all over it. We then wrote a wish for the coming year somewhere on the boat and all lined up on one side of the pool. If our boat made it across the pool, the wish would come true! I'm happy to report that mine made it across without incident, but we had to fetch the pool skimmer net for some of the unfortunate others.

If it's a small group, have them make their own origami boats, otherwise it might be best to make a bunch of them in advance so you don't have to re-explain the directions a bunch of times. Provide markers, metallic pens, stickers, and other decorations for the boats, and when the group has finished decorating their masterpieces, have them include a wish and have a race of your own. Swishing your hands in the water to get the boats moving is fine, but no fair jumping into the pool! Even if some become waterlogged and sink to the bottom, if you pull them up carefully they will dry out just fine and everyone can take his boat home. Night celebrations can use a small candle (like a tealight) in each boat for added excitement.

Gold Panning

Here in the Mother Lode of California's Sierra Nevada mountains, gold was everything in the 1850s. People killed, robbed, starved, and left everything they loved behind in the pursuit of the magical sun-colored metal that never tarnishes. Gold has long been one of the most important metals in the history of humankind, if not the most important. The ancient Egyptians likened gold to the sun god Ra, and used massive quantities of it in their funerary items, jewelry, statues, rituals, and daily life. The pre-Columbian South Americans, such as the Aztecs, Incas, and Maya, also used gold in exquisitely detailed objects for their royal god-kings. Europeans have also virtually worshipped the precious metal, using fine gold embroidery threads to decorate the vestments of Christian clergy since medieval times, and gilding everything that can be gilded in the houses of the aristocracy.

If you live in an area that produces gold, perhaps you've even tried panning for gold yourself a bit. It's an odd feeling, one of elation and almost an odd sort of déjà vu when you see the bright yellow bits of real gold shining up at you from the darkness of the gold pan. The raw metal is almost too golden—it doesn't look real at first—since it's not mixed with any other metal to make a jeweler's alloy. When you see the pure and perfect yellow gold you squint at it, making sure you're really seeing what you think you're seeing, and you understand why people have craved it so much since time immemorial.

Gold panning on the summer solstice seems especially appropriate to me. Gather enough pans for everyone, or have people pair up—one person shovels and one person pans. Also supply small bottles or vials filled with water for collecting any gold flakes you find. Look for a site on the bank of a creek or river where bedrock is exposed. This means that the riverbed is relatively shallow and it will be easier to dig down to the heavy gold-bearing sand at the bottom. Pull any large rocks out of the way and dig down with a small shovel until you start reaching black, iron-rich sand. Put a heap of this dark sand in your pan and dip it into the water. Gripping the edges of the pan like a steering wheel, hold it level and spin it back and forth to settle the heavier gold flakes to the bottom of the pan.

This part takes a bit of practice, but it's not that hard to do. Carefully swirl the pan full of sand and water so that the lighter pieces of sand and gravel flip out over the rim, leaving the dark iron-rich sand and gold at the bottom. Pick out any larger rocks and add more water, swirling carefully until the bottom of the pan is just covered with the remaining fine minerals. If you're lucky and the sun smiles upon you, you may see some tiny flakes of bright yellow gold in the bottom of your pan.

Pour out the excess water carefully and pick out the gold flakes. You should be able to stick them to your wet fingertip easily and touch them to the surface of the water in your vial, where the gold will fall to the bottom and collect in a most satisfying manner. Keep in mind that the water in the vial magnifies what's inside! When you're done, don't forget to replace any large rocks and give thanks for the precious gift that's been given to you.

CRAFTS

Litha Stitchery

A medieval-style sunburst shines brightly on the sky-blue fabric, metallic and rayon fibers adding sparkle and sheen. (For additional stitchery instructions and suggestions, see pages 211–214.)

Grid Size:	47 W × 47 H	
Cloth Count:	18	
Fabric:	Sky blue Aida	
Design Area:	2.61″ W × 2.61″ H (45 × 45 stitches)	

Pattern Key

Symbol	DMC Floss		Color
·	5200	(rayon, 1 strand)	Snow white
⁄⁄	972	(2 strands)	Canary—deep
▲	444	(2 strands)	Lemon—dark
♦	920	(2 strands)	Copper—medium
	Kreinik		
—	091	(1 strand)	Star yellow #4 braid

Backstitches

Symbol	DMC Floss		Color
———	920	(1 strand)	Copper—medium
------	608	(1 strand)	Bright orange

Note: Stitch the white rayon threads first, since they are slightly thicker and more difficult to work with than regular floss.

Sun Pinwheels

Pinwheels, in various forms, go back to at least medieval times. They are easy to make and can be decorated however you like to catch both the wind and the sun. If you're having an outdoor ritual, have each participant make one and stick the dowel into the ground behind them, creating a circle of pinwheels to work your magic inside.

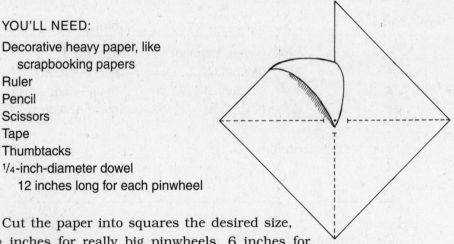

YOU'LL NEED:

Decorative heavy paper, like
   scrapbooking papers
Ruler
Pencil
Scissors
Tape
Thumbtacks
$\frac{1}{4}$-inch-diameter dowel
   12 inches long for each pinwheel

Cut the paper into squares the desired size, $8\frac{1}{2}$ inches for really big pinwheels, 6 inches for medium, and 4 inches for small. On the white side of the paper (if it is only decorated on one side), draw two lines from corner to corner, forming a large X. Find the center and measure out about 1 inch in all four directions, making a little pencil mark. Cut on the lines toward the center until you reach the mark. Lay the paper so that it looks like a diamond and fold the left side of the top corner so that it touches the center plus $\frac{1}{2}$ inch. This will make the pinwheel turn clockwise—if you'd like it to turn the other way, fold the right side down. Repeat with the other four corners until you have a classic pinwheel shape, and secure the center with a small square of tape. Push a thumbtack through the center of the tape so that it catches all four tips securely and goes through the back. Press the tack securely into the dowel about $\frac{1}{2}$ inch down from the top of one end.

Origami Boats

Make your own wish-filled boat out of colorful paper and watch it sail! These are easy to fold and fun to decorate however you like—see one example in the second photo insert. If you're having a dragon boat race, don't forget to draw on a dragon head!

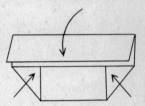

YOU'LL NEED:

Origami paper in whatever size you like
Metallic pens
Assorted markers
Stickers

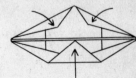

Make all folds as crisp as possible, using the side of a pen if necessary to press down the fold. Place the paper colored side up on a clean, flat table. Begin by folding the paper in half both directions, then unfolding it. This gives you a crease so that it's easy to tell where the exact center is. Now fold two sides of the paper so that the edges meet in the center. Now fold all four corners toward the center. Fold the four top and bottom corners toward the center again as shown—this fold will not go all the way in to touch the center, and the two folds meet in the middle of the boat wall (the second crease). Fold the final top and bottom points toward the center. Find the center and very carefully turn the whole boat inside out so that the colored side faces out and the inside of the boat is white. Now decorate and race your boat!

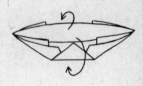

Note: If you're having problems with the paper tearing, try using a less stiff paper. For example, I found that crisp, decorative scrapbooking papers were hard to work with, but an old piece of junk mail from the recycling box worked out beautifully. Another tip for turning the boat is to push on the bottom corners (the ones you made with the last fold) and don't worry about crumpling up the paper a little as you turn the boat inside out. It flattens out just fine.

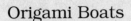

Sun-Dried Litha Potpourri

There's no mystery to making potpourri, and you can create your own blends for gift giving, party favors, or to tuck into your linens. By drying the flower petals in the sun, you will also be charging them with its solar powers, so this potpourri is especially good for lifting your mood and bringing balance to the home.

YOU'LL NEED:

24-inch-square window screen or equivalent
2 cups rose petals, any color
1 cup St. John's wort flower petals
1 cup sunflower petals
1 cup lavender flower heads
1 cup carnation petals
1 orange or lemon, sliced very thinly into wheels
Large mixing bowl
2 tablespoons powdered dried orris root
Several drops gardenia or freesia oil
Several drops cedar oil
A few drops rose oil
Large jar with an airtight lid

Lay the window screen in a sunny location, preferably out of any potentially windy area. A piece of fabric laid on the ground will also work, but the screen will dry the floral material faster and more evenly. Spread out all the flower petals and the citrus slices on the screen so that air can surround all the pieces evenly. If a breeze comes up, you'll need to lay another screen on top to keep the petals from blowing away.

After several hours, begin to check the dryness of the smaller petals—they should be papery dry but not brittle. Turn and/or sift through the petals and citrus slices with your fingers every few hours to ensure even drying and prevent them from sticking to the screen. Remove petals that are dry and keep checking every few hours. The larger petals and citrus slices may take up to several days to dry completely, depending on your weather.

When all the plant material is completely dry, mix it all together in a large bowl. Add the orris root and oils and mix them in completely so that the potpourri is evenly mixed and the oils are well distributed throughout the floral material. Use as much or as little of the oils as you like and even change them completely if you like other fragrances better. Citrus oils, for example, may be a good choice if you don't like florals. Seal your potpourri in an airtight jar to finish blending until ready to use in bowls and sachets throughout the house. It also makes a terrific gift and would be a wonderful solstice memento for your guests.

Sun Pictures

Perhaps you made some of these pictures when you were a kid, and they're just as much fun to make now. Have your guests select a pretty leaf, an interesting stick, some jewelry, or other objects and you'll have a "snapshot" of your Litha ritual.

YOU'LL NEED:

Heliographic (literally "sun print") paper
Various objects
Watch or clock
Plastic tub of water

Gather together your objects before taking the light-sensitive paper out of its envelope. Things that make interesting pictures are detailed leaves (fern, acacia, etc.), larger sculptural leaves (oak, maple, evergreens, etc.), transparent or translucent objects like glass, paper cutouts of shapes (sun, moon, etc.), and so on. Lay the heliographic paper in a sunny spot and quickly place the objects on it artistically. Practice your layout first on another piece of paper if you like. Let everything sit without disturbing the objects for the length of time indicated on the paper package instructions. To preserve the image, plunge the paper into a water bath to stop the chemical reaction and "freeze" the developing process. Make the paper into note cards, frame it, use it in scrapbooking projects, make origami . . . have fun with the fascinating image you've created.

Faerie Houses and Furniture

Tiny pixies appreciate a shady place to hide when the summer sun gets too hot, and you'll have great fun making one for them. Pick a spot in your garden that you think the faeries might like, such as a ferny nook or at the base of a tree where diminutive flowers grow, and don't forget to leave out some milk for them!

YOU'LL NEED:

Several pieces of flat slate stones
Assorted twigs, pinecone scales, nuts, seed pods, acorn caps,
   other plant materials
Utility knife
Glue gun

Construct the faerie house by partially burying two slates upright for the side walls (disturb as little of the earth as possible). Add one small slate to the back for a partial third wall, and lay a larger slate on top for the roof. If you want a more refined look, glue twigs together side-by-side on a piece of cardboard and use them to dress up the side walls or to form the back wall and a front wall with a rectangular hole for the front door. If you'd like the faeries to stay over the winter, you'll need to provide a front door and windows too. Glue together a wood frame and insert a tiny piece of glass, covering all the exposed edges with glue for safety.

Now you'll need to furnish the house. You might want to get some pictures of gypsy willow branch furniture or other rustic wooden furniture to work from if you feel a bit lost. Use your imagination and make furniture from twigs cut to length—simply attach the pieces with your glue gun rather than screws or nails. Make bed frames, chairs, benches, tables, and so on with the plant materials, trying to see each piece of material as potential furniture or accessories in miniature. Acorn caps turn into bowls, pine cone scales become chair seats, seed pods become vases, and so on. You can even make miniature picture frames and set little images inside that you think the faeries might like. Just work slowly and let the spirits of the land speak to you.

Barbecue (BYOM—Bring Your Own Meat)

Corn on the Cob

Summer Fruit Tray With Honey-Yogurt Sauce

Pele Bread

Tea-Poached Fruit

Fresh Honey Lemonade

Summer Fruit Tray With Honey-Yogurt Rose Sauce

When the days are too hot to eat a heavy meal, sometimes the perfect solution is simply a platter of delicious summer fruits, spread out attractively and served with a cool, sweet dip. Rose water, the secret ingredient that will have people asking you for the sauce recipe, is available in Middle Eastern food stores.

1 red apple, cored and sliced

1 green apple, cored and sliced

2 freestone peaches, pitted and sliced

2 freestone nectarines, pitted and sliced

6 apricots, pitted and sliced into quarters

6 firm plums, pitted and sliced

1/2 pound strawberries, hulled and cut in half

1/4 pound green seedless grapes on stems

1/4 pound red seedless grapes on stems

HONEY-YOGURT ROSE SAUCE

6 ounces vanilla yogurt	1/2 teaspoon cinnamon
1/2 cup honey	Pinch nutmeg
2 tablespoons rose water	

Wash and arrange the fruit on a large round tray, making stripes of color that radiate out from the center and leaving a hole in the middle. Place the Honey-Yogurt Rose Sauce in a bowl at the center of the tray, garnishing it with a few rose petals. Serve with toothpicks on the side if desired. 8–12 servings.

Pele Bread

Named for the Hawaiian goddess of fire, this spicy treat features tropical gingerroot in three different ways, and even has sweet maraschino cherry "embers" inside. Watch out—this bread may bite back!

3 cups flour	1 teaspoon vanilla
1 cup sugar	1/2 teaspoon lemon juice
4 teaspoons baking powder	1/3 cup peeled and finely minced
2 teaspoons powdered dry ginger	fresh gingerroot
1 teaspoon salt	10-ounce jar maraschino cherries,
1/2 cup shortening	drained and patted dry
1/2 cup butter	1/8 cup finely minced candied
1 1/2 cups milk	ginger
1 egg, beaten	

Preheat oven to 350 degrees F., grease and flour large (5 × 9-inch) loaf pan. In a large mixing bowl, combine dry ingredients. Cut in shortening and butter. In a medium mixing bowl, combine milk, egg, vanilla, lemon juice, and fresh ginger. Add to dry ingredients and mix until just blended. Stir in cherries. Spread batter evenly in loaf pan and sprinkle candied ginger on top. Bake for about an hour or until center tests done. Let cool completely before turning out and cutting. This is a very soft and moist bread, so cut thick slices and handle it as little as possible to prevent crumbling. Makes one loaf.

Tea-Poached Fruit

Serve over ice cream, whipped cream, crème fraîche, marscapone cheese, or vanilla custard.

1 cup dried apple rings, cut into quarters	¼ cup rose water
1 cup dried pear halves, coarsely chopped	5 whole cloves
1 cup apple juice	¼ teaspoon nutmeg
½ cup water	2 bags Celestial Seasonings After Dinner Tea, either English Toffee or Vanilla Hazelnut
½ cup sugar	

Combine all ingredients except the tea bags in a medium saucepan, stirring to blend thoroughly. Over medium-high heat, bring the mixture to a boil, stirring occasionally. Reduce the heat to low and simmer, covered, until the fruit is tender, about 20 minutes. Add the tea bags and simmer another two minutes, then remove from heat. Allow to stand another minute and remove the tea bags. Strain the fruit, reserving the liquid, and discard the whole cloves, then prepare the plates with ice cream or whatever you will be serving with the fruit. Sprinkle the fruit on top of the ice cream, etc. and drizzle with a tablespoon of the hot apple juice mixture. 4–6 servings.

Fresh Honey Lemonade

This is true old-fashioned lemonade at its best. Once you taste this, you'll never want to go back to the store-bought kind!

5 lemons	1 cup boiling water
1 cup sugar	4 cups ice water
1 cup honey	

Wash the lemons, cut them in half, and juice them. Strain out any seeds and set aside the juice. In a large bowl, place the used lemon halves, add sugar, and mix, making sure the lemons are evenly coated with sugar. Drizzle with honey. Allow to stand ½ hour (any longer and the lemonade will turn out bitter). Pour boiling water over the peels and stir until the sugar and honey are dissolved. Add the reserved lemon juice and ice water and stir well. Add water or sugar to taste. You may leave the lemon rinds in the juice if it is to be served immediately or remove them if your lemonade will be served later. Makes about 48 ounces or more, depending on how strong you like it.

DECORATIONS

Sunflowers: Few flowers say "summer" to me than the sunflower. Whether wild multi-branched clusters of smaller blooms or a single gigantic seed-producing head, the humble sunflower deserves a place on the altar and around the house. Fill cobalt blue pitchers with smaller cutting sunflowers in a rainbow of colors. Lay a huge seed-filled bloom in the center of a round table as a centerpiece. Make a hanging sphere of the yellow blossoms, just like a kissing ball (page 20), by plunging the stems into wet floral foam. Now matter how you use them, these sunny flowers reflect the day perfectly.

Roses: One of the summer's most glorious blooms, the rose is the perfect decorating accent. This flower, popular since the Dark Ages with commoners and royalty alike, has been bred to display a dizzying array of colors, shapes, sizes, textures, fragrances, and foliage. Twist rambling climbing roses together into a rope and hang the swags all over the place! Cut stems in vases add beauty and class to any situation—try using an entire row of bud vases along the back of your buffet table, filled with as many different kinds of roses as you can find for an attractive riot of blooms.

Sun hangings and lights: If you're lucky, you may be able to find sun-shaped patio lights at your local party supply store or on the Internet. Mix them with golden sun-shaped Yule ornaments, homemade cut paper adornments, and honeycomb tissue-paper decorations.

Candles: Use yellow or gold holders to give an even sunnier impression of bright candle flames. Many people don't think of using candles in the summer, but as reflections of the Sun King, any kind of fire is appropriate for the summer solstice. The candles don't need to be restricted to just yellow or gold—use a mass of candles in all shapes, sizes and colors for a chaotic display sure to make your guests smile.

Summer stonefruits: The summer fruits are at their peak or close to it. Decorate with large glass bowls filled with cherries, plums, peaches, apricots, and any other delectable seasonal fruits you can procure. What's even better, your company will be able to enjoy eating the decorations while they celebrate.

Watermelons: Whether edible or ceramic, no summer would be complete without watermelons. The colorful (and huge) fruits make great decorations when whole, cut into wedges and placed on ice, or made into a basket and filled with fruit salad. Bright red and green ceramic melon bowls are a good way to add color and whimsy to the buffet table, and if you collect watermelon-motif items, now's the perfect time to get them all out.

Metallic gold tableware: Use as many brass and gold-colored items as you can on the table, including the tablecloth, serving platters, vases, napkins, flatware, plates, cups, and so on. Gold tableware is available at most party supply stores, especially if they carry anniversary or wedding lines of goods.

Images of the Oak King, Holly King, sun deities like Ra and Amaterasu

6

LUGHNASSADH/LAMMAS

(August 1–6)

The moment is right and they walk out into the golden fields, sickles and scythes in hand. John Barleycorn must die. In the distance one of the older boys plays a simple tune on a polished bone flute. The people begin to sing together as they cut the stalks of grain and bundle them into neat sheaves, twisting lengths of straw together as crude ropes to hold the bundles together. The first of the grains to be cut is made into a tall corn dolly, the Goddess of the harvest, and it is she that will preside over that night's feast of the first harvest.

The grain is dry enough to be ground into a fine flour, perhaps by hand, perhaps by horses or water turning a heavy millstone. Sea salt, fresh water from the spring, yeast collected from wild grape skins and the freshly ground flour are all assembled. Then the baker begins her work. She warms the water over the wood fire and mixes all the ingredients together, then kneads the dough until it is strong and springs back when touched. She forms the dough into a great round loaf, marks it with sacred symbols, and places it in the oven, the hot coals having been swept to each side for even baking. She hums and smiles as she washes her hands, knowing that this first loaf of bread will be honored at the harvest ceremonies tonight.

The name "Lammas" is the shortened version of Christianity's "Loaf Mass." This ancient agricultural cross-quarter holiday celebrates the harvest of the first grain and the making of the first loaves of bread. But grain is not the only thing harvested this time of year, with many berries, fruits and nuts coming ripe as well. Home canners know that this is a prime season for "putting up," or making preserves (despite the heat). The kitchens of the world are gearing up, and Lammas is opening night of the harvest season's bountiful show.

For the Celts, the holiday is also in honor of Lugh, a popular hero of the Tuatha de Dannan, as well as Crom Dubh, "the bent and dark one." Lugh, "the shining one," is considered both a sun god and god of the grain, and some say that Lughnassadh is the day that the sun's energy goes into the grain. Crom Dubh emerges from the underworld on August 1, stooped over from carrying heavy sheaves of grain to mankind. It's easy to see the polarity of these two gods, both honored on Lughnassadh, and it's reminiscent of the Oak King and Holly King duality.

Bread, and the grain from it are the central focus of this day, the first of our three harvest holidays. Throughout the history of humankind, grains and bread have been central to survival, whether the unleavened loaves that saw the Jews out of Egypt or the hardtack that fed many an American sailor and soldier in the nineteenth century. Just as European Pagans honor the God as the spirit of the grain, giving of himself so that we may eat, so, too, do the Native Americans honor Corn Mother, the Asiatic peoples honor Rice Mother, the Ancient Egyptians (and Kemetics today) honor Neper and Amsu, and on and on throughout the world.

John Barleycorn Must Die

John Barleycorn is another European grain character, one that causes a bit of confusion over the use of corn in some modern rituals. Corn, to Europeans, means any kind of grain, so Barleycorn speaks of the barley grain, not what we usually think of as "corn" today, which is native American maize. This personification of barley was made especially famous in The Ballad of John Barleycorn written by Robert Burns in the eighteenth century, but there is an older version that goes like this:

There were three men come from the West
Their fortunes for to try,
And these three made a solemn vow:
"John Barleycorn must die."

They plowed, they sowed, they harrowed him in,
Threw clods upon his head,
'Til these three men were satisfied
John Barleycorn was dead.

They let him lie for a very long time,
'Til the rains from heaven did fall,
When little Sir John raised up his head
And so amazed them all.

They let him stand 'til Midsummer's Day
When he looked both pale and wan;
Then little Sir John grew a long, long beard
And so became a man.

They hired men with their scythes so sharp
To cut him off at the knee;
They rolled him and tied him around the waist,
And served him barbarously.

They hired men with their sharp pitchforks
To pierce him to the heart,
But the loader did serve him worse than that,
For he bound him to the cart.

They wheeled him 'round and around the field
'Til they came unto a barn,
And there they took a solemn oath
On poor John Barleycorn.

They hired men with their crab-tree sticks
To split him skin from bone,
But the miller did serve him worse than that,
For he ground him between two stones.

There's little Sir John in the nut-brown bowl,
And there's brandy in the glass,
And little Sir John in the nut-brown bowl
Proved the strongest man at last.

The huntsman cannot hunt the fox
Nor loudly blow his horn
And the tinker cannot mend his pots
Without John Barleycorn.

There is a tune that goes along with the poem, making it a popular song for performing at harvest rituals. The tune is available on the Internet and in *Hugin the Bard's Book of Pagan Songs*.

As the ballad illustrates, the Green Man under the alias of Sir John Barleycorn raises up his head after being considered dead and buried, grows a beard and becomes a man as the grass lengthens, then is killed again as he ripens and is harvested. It's the classic tale of the life of the god of grain retold in a humorous and very entertaining way.

Processing Grains for Food

A great project for yourself, your family and/or your coven is to grow the wheat (or any other grain) yourself for the Lughnassadh bread. It takes less space than you think—just a few square feet is all you need to grow enough wheat for a large loaf of bread. In the spring after it's warmed up a bit, till the land where you plan to grow your wheat so that it's fine, crumbly, and free of very large dirt clods. Don't overtill, which is especially easy to do with large machine tillers. Scatter the seeds over the tilled plot by hand, rake the area gently, and pat down lightly to snug the seeds into the soil—this deters birds and mice as well as ensuring good soil contact. Now simply let nature have her way with the seeds, and soon you'll have a lush patch of wheat grass.

Allow the grains to ripen, watering only if you hit a dry spell before the heads form. You don't want the drying heads of grain to get wet or they could spoil. Watch the ripening heads carefully as they turn golden yellow, checking to see when the grains have dried and hardened fully. The grains should be too hard to dent with your thumbnail, but not so dry that they "shatter" out of their husks. Make sure to harvest your wheat before the brittle shatter stage or you'll loose a lot of kernels before you can thresh and winnow them.

Harvest the wheat with a scythe or other long, sharp blade and gather the grass stalks into bundles as you work. Prepare a tarp, blanket, garage floor, or other clean, flat surface and spread the wheat out on it. You'll need to thresh the wheat to separate the grain kernels from the chaff, which is discarded or composted. You can use many methods to thresh the wheat, including walking over it, beating the bundles on the ground, or using a traditional flail. It's easy to make a flail by connecting two stout sticks with a short length of rope, rather like martial arts nunchuks but with one half serving as a long handle to the shorter stick half. The Egyptian flail uses three beating sticks tied to one long handle stick.

After the grain is threshed, you'll need to winnow away everything that's not edible. You can do this by pouring the grain into a large bowl or bucket on a windy day, and pouring it from this container to another container, allowing the wind to blow away any grass stems, chaff, unformed grains, and so on. Another method is to use a flat, tightly woven basket and flip a portion of wheat up into the air, allowing the chaff to blow away while you catch the grains back on the basket. Keep winnowing until all of the wheat is clean and ready to grind into flour.

Grinding the grain is easily done with a hand grinder. These metal human-powered machines with a crank handle clamp onto a tabletop and produce a surprising amount of flour in a short amount of time (especially if you have all your coveners help out). If you're impatient, however, and plan to make quite a lot of flour, you may want to invest in an electric grain mill. Both types of mills are adjustable and can process everything from coarse cornmeal to very fine baking flour.

Bread Making

Bread is one of the most ancient foods known, and has been a staple of life since before recorded history. As the next stage in the life of the harvested grain, bread and bread making feeds the body as well as the spirit. Some cultures believe that their creator deity made the first people from bread dough. Unleavened bread is an important symbol to the Jews, especially at Passover, which is also known as Hag ha-Mazot, or "the feast of unleavened bread." The Indians of the American Southwest and Southeast honor Corn Mother, and much of their ceremonial life centers around the growing, honoring, and eating of corn. Christianity honors bread as the body of Christ in the eucharist ceremony. And of course, we honor bread as the body of the God who has sacrificed himself so that we may eat and live.

There is something uniquely tactile about making bread. It used to be such a commonplace affair that nearly everyone made bread at home, but we "modern" people have lost the knowledge and familiarity with this process for the most part. It's very unusual to eat fresh bread right from the oven, and although people mostly admire that I make it on occasion, sometimes they look at me like I'm some sort of alien and say ". . . Why?" And I look back at them with pity. They wouldn't be saying that if they'd ever tasted fresh, homemade bread.

It actually goes beyond just eating the nice fresh warm loaves. It's the connection to something utterly ancient that has remained largely unchanged for thousands of years. It's the sensation of handling the raw dough and the meditation of kneading it until it's springy and strong. It's watching the invisible yeast do amazing things under the cloth that covers the bread bowl. It's tapping on a rich brown crust to listen and see if the loaf is done, just as my ancestors did further back than I can trace them. The feeling of satisfaction and connection. That's why I make bread.

One way of getting everyone involved with making bread at your next gathering is to give them a little piece of the dough to knead and shape into a bun. Alternately, you can give each person a bit of the job—one could mix the yeast into the warm water, one could measure out the ingredients, one could prepare the pans, and so on. Children are also fascinated with making bread, although the length of time it takes to rise should be spent with other activities so they don't lose interest. Just make sure your ingredients are fresh, that all participants have thoroughly washed their hands, and you're ready for the rush when everyone wants a piece of fresh bread hot from the oven.

Market Faire

The harvest season is also a popular time to have a market faire. In England, a giant stuffed glove is paraded through the streets until it comes to rest over the faire, the symbol of the trustworthy handshake reminding shoppers and merchants alike to give each other a fair and truthful deal. Have your own faire and have all your guests bring things they have made or grown to trade or sell to each other. Even things like used children's clothing, books, or the offer of a massage on the spot would be good ideas for your market. Don't forget your giant glove! You could put it on your invitations, on a banner over the gate, or make one out of fabric and hang it from a long pole over the festivities.

Corn Shucking

It's not the most glamorous task to pull the husks off of ears of corn, but a shucking party can be great fun when you really get into it. This works well for both dried corns like popcorn and for green sweet corns. Have some of your party play lively music if you have a talented bardic bunch or used recorded songs, and provide large containers for both the finished corn and the husks. It's a relatively easy and "mind-less" chore, so you can choose to sing along with the music, sing sacred songs without accompaniment, tell stories, or just visit with each other. Be sure to save the husks for making dolls! Lay them out in the sun to dry if the husks are green, or pile them in a cloth or burlap sack if they're papery dry.

If you happen to have dried corns such as popcorn or flint corn for making cornmeal, you can also choose to take the kernels off the cobs (also called shucking). Use leather gloves and twist your hands along the cobs over a wide bowl to catch the dried kernels. Alternately, if you have a very large amount to be shucked, you can get a simple hand shucker or get a spiffy automatic shucker. (See Resources) I love old-timey inventions, and it's endless fun to feed the ears of dried corn into the hole and watch the empty cobs fall out the other hole while the kernels pour into a bowl underneath the contraption. Later, after the work is done, make a giant bowl of popcorn for everyone to enjoy.

The Wicker Man

So who is the Wicker Man and why do we burn him? There are two traditions that go along with this ancient practice, one at Beltane and one at Lammas. At Beltane, the Wicker Man (a large effigy made of woven branches) is burned and the ashes used to fertilize the fields. The Lammas Wicker Man is symbolic of the God of the Grain and the yearly sacrifice of his body so that we may eat. There are also traditions that burn the Wicker Man at Mabon and at Samhain, and the now famous Burning Man Festival (not directly Pagan but an obvious offshoot of the Wicker Man) is held every year around Labor Day weekend in the Nevada desert.

If you would like to incorporate the tradition of the Wicker Man into your harvest festivities, you'll need several things. First, you'll need a permit from the fire department to burn large things in your yard or the ability to use an outdoor firepit for a smaller Wicker Man. Second, you'll need a Wicker Man to burn, his size based on where and how you are able to burn things on your property. Third, you'll need things to place inside the effigy, such as notes from each participant that describes something good they've harvested over the last year, stuff from the altar that needs to be gotten rid of respectfully, and so on. Lastly, you'll need fire safety equipment, such as shovels, a garden hose, a bucket of sand, etc., to be sure you don't violate local laws or otherwise get your name in the newspapers.

Let's assume you're able to burn a life-size (5–6 feet high) Wicker Man on your property. A simple way to make one is to tie a very large, 5–6-foot-long bundle of branches together in the middle for the body, dividing the bundle in half for the legs, which are tied at the ankles with heavy string. Use a large wad of newspaper in the middle to hold the middle out and as kindling. Trim the bundle at the top to make shoulders, leaving branches in the middle for the head. Tie the bundle at the neck securely and trim the top of the head to shape. For arms, make two more small tapering bundles about 2½ feet long, tying them tightly at both ends. Butt up the arms to the shoulders and tie them on tightly, weaving the string throughout the body and arm to attach them well. Alternately, you can make a "Blair Witch"–type frame (a large **X** with a crosspiece on top for the arms) and cover it with bundles of twigs.

In your chosen location, drive two lengths of metal rebar into the ground and secure the legs onto these so your Wicker Man stands upright. Make sure he's well secured so he doesn't flop over dangerously when burning. Also make sure your burning area has been cleared of everything and a circle of rocks has been placed in a wide circle around the figure. When all is ready, you can adorn your man with a wreath of grain and/or flowers and have your participants tuck written prayers, wishes, little charms, items from the altar, or other things inside him. Preferably at night for maximum effect, light the center of the Wicker Man using a taper candle (which doesn't blow out as easily as a match) and stand back. Hold hands, sing songs, send up prayers, share what you've harvested this year, and watch the Wicker Man burn.

CRAFTS

Lammas Stitchery

The first grains have been brought in, and the first loaf has been made. Enjoy this permanent reminder of a temporal holiday, with some accents rendered in variegated floss. (For additional stitchery instructions and suggestions, see pages 211–214.)

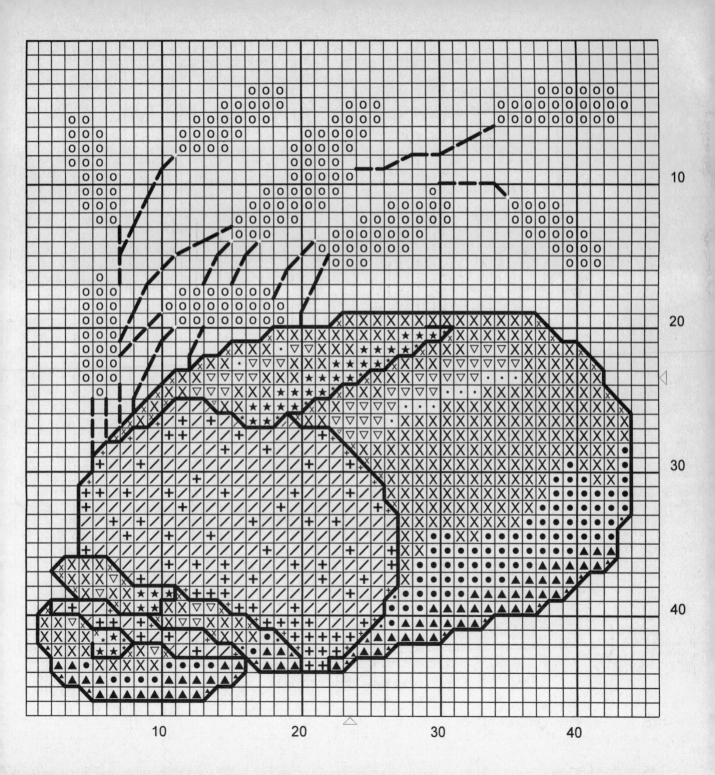

Grid Size: 47 W × 47 H
Cloth Count: 18
Fabric: Sage Aida
Design Area: 2.61″ W × 2.61″ H (43 × 43 stitches)

Pattern Key

Symbol	DMC Floss		Color
▲	433	(2 strands)	Brown—medium
•	434	(2 strands)	Brown—light
X	435	(2 strands)	Brown—very light
/	739	(2 strands)	Tan—very light
+	676	(2 strands)	Old gold—light
·	White	(2 strands)	White
★	437	(2 strands)	Tan—light
▽	111 + 676	(1 strand each)	Variegated mustard & old gold—light

Backstitches

Symbol	DMC Floss		Color
——	300	(1 strand)	Mahogany—very dark
- - -	3822	(3 strands)	Straw—light

Note: Stitch the 3-strand grain stems before the other backstitching. See the following chart for the grain-heads backstitching.

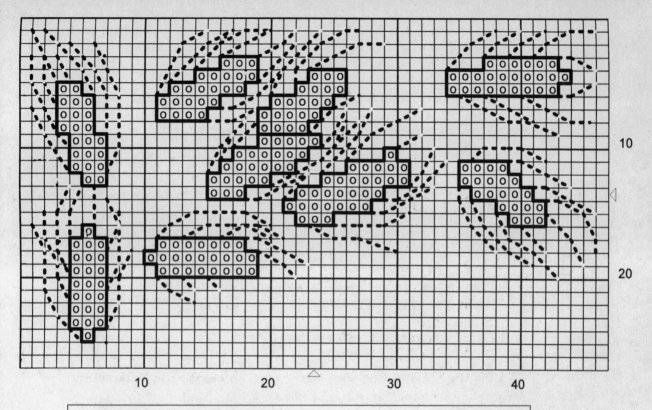

Grid Size: 47 W × 27 H
Cloth Count: 18
Fabric: Aida
Design Area: 2.61″ W × 1.5″ H (45 × 24 stitches)

Pattern Key

Symbol	DMC Floss	Color
o	61 + 111 (1 strand each)	Variegated topaz & variegated mustard

Backstitches

Symbol	DMC Floss	Color
——	300 (1 strand)	Mahogany—very dark
- - -	61 (1 strand)	Variegated golden brown

Corn Dolly

Although called "corn dollies," these woven figures of the Lady of the Harvest are usually made of wheat or similar grains ("corn" being a European term for grain in general, not American maize), and are not used as toys. Often made with the first or last sheaf of wheat harvested, this goddess blesses the fields to assure next year's bounty and is often kept in the house to bless it as well. The next year she is burned in the bonfire that takes the Wicker Man or in other harvest bonfires and the cycle begins again.

YOU'LL NEED:

Wallpaper soaking tray

Large bundle of wheat stalks (or other grain grasses)

Wheat-colored embroidery floss

Scissors

Fabric scraps and ribbons for clothing (optional)

Fill the soaking tray with warm water and soak the stalks of the wheat until completely soft and pliable (from 15 minutes to 2 hours, depending on the variety of wheat). Test the straws for flexibility—if they crack when bent double, they're not ready.

Set aside nine stalks and leave them soaking. With the floss, tie the other straws into a bundle just below the heads of grain to form the head of the figure. Cut the heads off the nine stalks plus about 3 inches of straw and set aside. Tie the nine headless straws into a bundle and slip this bundle up inside the body of the dolly with the floss tie in the middle. Tie off the body below the arms to form the waist of the dolly. Bend the arm stalks at the shoulder gently, then bend again about 2 inches down from there to form elbows. Bend again at another 2 inches to form wrists and tie these off with floss. Trim off the excess straw to within 1/2 inch of the wrist tie to make rounded hands.

Tie the nine heads of grain together to form a bouquet and tie this to the hands of the dolly. Arrange the body/dress straws of the figure below the waist where they are tied so they lay evenly in a neat bundle.

Trim off the bottom of the dress to form a flat base so the dolly can stand up. Dress and adorn the figure if desired.

Straw Pentacle Wreath

This wreath is easy to make and a lovely reminder of the season. It's a fun project for a whole group too, since everyone can help add something to the finished product.

YOU'LL NEED:

16-inch straw craft wreath
Measuring tape
Large paperclip (optional)
Glue gun and glue sticks
Marker
5 sticks at least 12 inches long
1 large bundle of dried wheat or other grains
1 small bundle mixed dried grasses
Assortment of dried flowers
Dried fruits and seed pods, such as pomegranates, citrus slices,
     poppy pods, etc.

Start by gently knocking or tapping the wreath outside to get rid of as many loose straw bits as possible. Measure the inside circumference of the straw wreath. Divide this measurement by five, and then find the exact top. If the wreath has no hanger, make a **U**-shape from a large paperclip, bend the ends back about 1/2 inch, and dig the bent ends firmly up into the straw to form a hanger. Use glue to secure it. Mark the inside of the wreath at the exact top, then mark off the four other equal measurements, dividing the wreath into five sections. Hold the sticks up to the top and lower left mark, cutting them to length as needed. Glue the sticks inside the wreath in the form of a pentagram, interweaving them and placing the ends on the marks made earlier.

When the sticks are secured and the glue is completely hardened, lay the wreath down and begin placing the grains on the top surface. Break or cut the straws below the grain heads to about 5 inches long and begin tacking them down with a bit of glue. Overlap the grains so that the heads hide the straws beneath. When you get back to where you started, tuck the final loose straws under the first heads and glue down. Now choose some attractive dried grasses and glue these in the same overlapping manner along the outside edge of the wreath. Do the same on the inside edge, but use less so that you don't obscure the pentacle design. Finally, add the dried flowers, fruits, and seed pods in random places all over the wreath, arranging them however it pleases you. You could also make little floral clusters here and there, or concentrate all the flowers and fruits in one large spray at the bottom.

When you're finished, remove all the glue "spiderwebs" and hang. This wreath is somewhat fragile, so be sure to pack it away carefully when not using it, perhaps in a specially-designed wreath storage box (usually available at large craft and variety stores). To clean the wreath, gently blow off any accumulated dust.

Harvest Time Pillow Packet Sachets

It's harvest time for many dried flowers too, and lavender is one of the best—it smells amazing, dries and keeps very well, and even helps keep moths away from your favorite linens. I always have some lavender growing in my gardens. The clever woven corn husk packets can be left natural tan or dyed any way you like with food dyes. You can also make this out of colorful paper for a Beltane favor.

YOU'LL NEED:

2 or 3 cornhusks cut into 1/2-inch-wide strips
Tacky craft glue
1/2 cup dried lavender flowers or about 15 whole dried lavender heads

Trim the harder butt ends off the corn husks if necessary so the remaining husks will lie flat and even. Lay out five strips on a flat surface. Weave five more into these strips so that you have a woven square. Push the strips as close together as possible to form a tight weave.

Fold the husk strip ends in half so that they all lie on top of the woven square. Make sure you fold them right on the edges of the square for a nicely enclosed finished packet. Glue the ends of five strips together going in one direction so that you have five flat parallel strips glued together and running across the packet. When the glue has dried, use your fingers to press on opposite sides of the packet so that a "mouth" opens up, something like a coin purse, and you can pour the lavender inside.

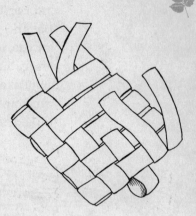

Now you'll be weaving the remaining strips to finish the packet. Beginning at one corner, look at whether the corner strip was inside or outside of the last one it wove through—if the strip was outside, weave it to the inside first. The same holds true if it was on the inside—weave it on the outside first. Now simply weave the strips in and out of the glued strips, tucking in the ends to lock them in place. Use your thumb to press the edges of the packet, forming a crisp fold. Trim off any excess husk ends if necessary.

Coiled Winnowing Basket

Coiled basketry is actually older than pottery vessels, and this is proved by the imprint of the coils left on the outside of the earliest known pots—the clay was worked inside shallow, bowl-shaped baskets. This basket can be made a number of ways and with a number of different coil foundation materials, including grasses, stems, pine needles, willow or other thin branch rods, or even fabric and wire. One of the easiest materials to find and use for this project is the willow rod, so that's what I selected for people who may have never made a coiled basket before.

YOU'LL NEED:

30 or more fresh willow branches
Pruning shears
1 or 2 packages of undyed raffia
Large blunt tapestry needle (like for needlepoint)
Knife or scissors

For tips on gathering good weaving willows, see the "Green Willow Basket" project in the Ostara chapter. Strip off all the leaves and snip off the very tips of the branches where there's nothing but one or two leaves hanging on.

Take several strands of raffia, perhaps six or seven, and tie a single overhand knot in the middle. Select one long, smooth strand of the raffia with no snags or rips and thread this through the tapestry needle.

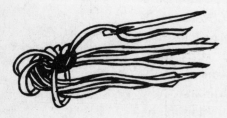

Push the needle through the center of the knot and "sew" the raffia through, pulling it snugly (but not too tightly) to finish. Smooth the rest of the raffia in the bundle where your stitching raffia came from and begin stitching over this bundle. Continue pushing the needle through the center of the knot as you work your way around from left to right, enclosing the bundle of raffia inside the one strand inside the needle. When you get to the other half of the raffia knot bundle, simply lay the other raffia over it and continue stitching over the raffia bundle.

When you reach the point where you began stitching, push the needle through the previous coil and continue until you begin to run out of raffia foundation and the coil becomes noticeably thinner. At this point, insert the thin end of a willow rod into the raffia bundle and continue to stitch. About an inch past that point, add another willow rod the same way. Then add a third rod in the same manner and begin to cut out raffia strands to make a smooth transition to the willow rod foundation. When you have come around to where there is only willow rods, stitch over all three rods and continue working. When working over the willow foundation, pull the raffia very tightly as you stitch.

As you work towards the outside edges of your basket, the stitches will become farther and farther apart. When the stitches are about an inch apart, start adding extra stitches so that they are never more than about an inch apart—this ensures that your basket is really strong when you're finished. Keep working, cutting the ends of the rods at an angle and adding new rods by pushing the thin tips into the bundle of rods. Don't let two rods end at the same point—always cut off a rod early if you need to. This will avoid weak spots in your finished basket.

To add new raffia, tuck a new strand inside the bundle and stitch over it for a few inches. When you're ready to switch, simply thread it through the needle and begin stitching with the new strand, tucking the old one into the bundle and stitching over it for a few more inches. Snip off the old strand when it and the new one are secure.

Keep weaving in a concentric spiral from the center, creating a basically flat disk with a slight bowl-shape to it. When the basket is about 16 inches across, cut off one of the rods at an angle and keep stitching. In another 6 inches, cut off the second rod and keep going with one rod. After another 6 inches, cut off the third rod and simply stitch until there's nothing left to wrap. To end off the raffia, push the needle back through the foundation going under several previous stitches (at least four or five). Pull it very tight and clip it off to end. You should now have a nice tight winnowing basket that can be held by the edges in both hands. Use it to toss your grains up into the air so that the breeze can blow away any chaff.

MENU

Seitan Quesadillas

Grain-Shaped Yeast Bread

Cheese Buns

Black Walnut Corn Muffins

Bread and Rice Pudding With Wild Blackberry Sauce

Soy Milk, Beer, Honey Mead

Seitan Quesadillas

Seitan is also called "wheat meat," and it can be used as a meat substitute in many recipes. In celebration of wheat, combine the Asian seitan with the Mexican flour tortilla, and you've got a new family favorite that's ridiculously easy to prepare.

4 large or 8 small flour tortillas	2 jalapeño peppers, seeded and
1/2 pound seitan, cut into strips	sliced or minced (optional)
1/4 pound sharp Cheddar cheese	Taco sauce or salsa (optional)
1/4 pound jack cheese	

Evenly distribute the seitan, cheeses, and peppers over half of each tortilla. Place a tortilla into a hot nonstick skillet or frying pan, fold in half, and place the lid on the pan. Cook for about 30 seconds or until tortilla begins to brown slightly on the bottom. Flip the tortilla over and cook until cheese is melted and the bottom begins to brown slightly. Cut into quarters and serve with hot sauce or salsa if desired. 8 servings.

Beltane

A beautiful—and edible—centerpiece for a Beltane celebration.

Litha

An origami dragon boat to fill with Litha wishes.

A gingery loaf of Pele bread is studded with cherry "embers."

Lammas

Cornhusk-and-lavender sachet unites the fragrance of summer with the crispness of autumn.

Mabon

A basket of cracked acorns and a bowl of acorn meats ready for drying and skinning.

From left to right: English walnuts still in their fragrant green hulls, partially dried, and ready to crack and eat.

A traditional and colorful corn ladder.

Collect fallen leaves in all the hues of autumn to make this "stained glass" window hanging.

Use shiny fresh fruit to make these novel candleholders for the Mabon table.

Samhain

A festive Samhain altar in honor of loved ones who have passed beyond the veil.

"Shrunken heads" freshly carved in preparation for drying.

Wheel of the Year wall-hanging.

Grain-Shaped Yeast Bread

Homemade fresh bread, hot out of the oven, can be a meal in itself. This gorgeous centerpiece is easier to make than you might think, and fits perfectly into any autumnal ritual or meal.

1¼ cups hot water	2 teaspoons salt
1 tablespoon yeast	About 4 cups whole-wheat flour
3 tablespoons vegetable oil	1 egg white, lightly beaten
2 tablespoons honey	¼ cup wheat germ

Pour ¼ cup of the hot (not boiling) water into a small bowl, and stir in the yeast. In a large ceramic bowl, combine the remaining water with the oil, honey, and salt with a wooden spoon. After the yeast is softened, pour it into the large bowl and mix together gently. Add the flour, one cup at a time, until the dough begins to come away from the sides of the bowl and it's difficult to stir. Turn the dough out onto a floured surface and knead about 10 minutes or until quite elastic. Knead into a long loaf shape and place on a nonstick or oiled cookie sheet.

With a very sharp knife, make several diagonal cuts in the sides of the loaf to form the individual kernels of wheat, pulling the tips of the cut portions into points. Make a slice on top of each kernel from base to tip. Cover with a clean towel and allow to rise in a warm place until doubled, about 30 minutes. The inside of your gas oven with just the pilot on or the top of your refrigerator are ideal. When the loaf has risen fully, brush the entire loaf with egg white. Sprinkle the wheat germ on the center of the loaf and the outside edges of the kernels, avoiding the middles where you made the slices. Bake the loaf at 375 degrees F. for about 35 minutes or until it forms a nice brown crust and sounds hollow when tapped in the center. Allow to cool about 10 minutes, then transfer the loaf to a wooden cutting board and serve warm with fresh butter.

Cheese Buns

Would you believe this creation is a favorite at my old high school's cafeteria? These beautiful brown buns with a cheesy surprise in the middle would sell out quickly, so it paid to be first in line.

1	tablespoon yeast	About 3 cups flour	
1/4	cup hot water	8	ounces mild Cheddar or American cheese, cut into 12 pieces
1/2	cup milk		
1/2	cup vegetable oil		
1	teaspoon salt	1	egg white, beaten slightly

In a small bowl, combine the yeast and water, and set aside. In a large bowl combine the milk, oil, and salt. When the yeast has softened, add it to the milk mixture and add the flour, stirring it in a cup at a time until it forms a dough that pulls away from the sides of the bowl and isn't too sticky to work with. Turn the dough out onto a floured surface and knead for about 5 minutes. Divide the dough into 12 equal portions, roll each one into a ball, and press the ball flat. Place a piece of cheese in the middle of each ball and fold the dough over it, pinching it closed and forming a ball once again. Place the balls, pinched side down, on a cookie sheet and cover. Allow to rise until almost doubled, about 45 minutes. Preheat the oven to 375 degrees F. and brush the buns with egg white while you're heating up the oven. Bake for about 15 minutes or until evenly browned. Cool at least 5 minutes before serving. Makes 12 large buns.

Golden Piñon Corn Muffins

This beautiful sun-colored treat features some interesting ingredients and can be served as a side dish, breakfast bread, after-school snack, or even as a dessert when drizzled with fresh orange honey. Make sure the flower petals you use are pesticide free and have been washed.

1 cup yellow cornmeal	1/4 cup butter, melted
3/4 cup flour	1/4 cup milk, warmed
1 tablespoon baking powder	1/4 cup maple syrup
1/2 teaspoon salt	1 cup pine nuts
1 egg, beaten	1/4 cup marigold or calendula petals

Preheat the oven to 400 degrees F. and prepare muffin cups either by spraying with pan spray or lining with cupcake papers and lightly spraying the papers. In a large bowl, combine the cornmeal, flour, baking powder, and salt. In a medium mixing bowl, combine the egg, butter, milk, and maple syrup. Add the liquid ingredients to the dry, stirring just until blended (batter will be lumpy). Add the pine nuts and marigold petals, stir to mix them in, and drop the batter into the cups with a couple of spoons. Bake for about 20–25 minutes or until lightly golden brown on the edges. Makes about 12 muffins.

Bread and Rice Pudding
With Wild Blackberry Sauce

What dessert could be more appropriate for Lammas than one featuring bread, grains, and the last of the summer fruits? The rich sauce is easy to make, and you may find yourself using it on lots of other dishes too.

3 cups fresh bread, cut into cubes	3/4 cup sugar
1 cup cooked white rice, preferably basmati	1/2 teaspoon vanilla
1/2 cup raisins	1/2 teaspoon salt
1 1/2 cups milk	Whipped cream
3 eggs, beaten	

FOR THE SAUCE
2 cups blackberries
1 cup honey

Spray a 9 × 13-inch baking dish lightly with cooking spray and preheat the oven to 350 degrees F. In a large bowl, toss the bread with the rice and raisins until blended, then evenly distribute the mixture into the prepared baking dish. In a medium bowl, combine the milk, eggs, sugar, vanilla, and salt. Pour this mixture over the bread mixture in the pan, teasing it with a fork to ensure that the milk mixture penetrates the contents of the pan. Bake the pudding for about 45 minutes or until the center tests done with a wooden toothpick.

While the pudding is baking, prepare the sauce. Mash the berries and press through a wire sieve to remove most of the seeds. Pour the berry mush into a medium pan and add the honey. Heat over medium-high until boiling, then reduce the heat to low and simmer, stirring frequently, for about 15–20 minutes or until the mixture has thickened and reduced. Serve the pudding with the blackberry sauce drizzled over the top and whipped cream on the side. 10–12 servings.

DECORATIONS

Wheat sheaves, weavings: A popular decorating accent at the moment is a small sheaf of wheat, bundled tightly together and trimmed at the bottom so that it stands up on its own. Place these on the table, mantelpiece, or buffet, "plant" them in clay flowerpots, or stand them on the altar. Other grain decorations, like woven wheat "dollies," cornucopias, and wreaths, are perfect seasonal accents for anywhere in the home or ritual space.

Corn stalks: Tall and friendly, a bundle of either green, freshly gathered cornstalks or brown, dried stalks look great on the front porch, especially when tied around old-fashioned porch posts. Corn stalks are also a fantastic way to flank your altar, indoors or out. If you can get them, try to find stalks with dried ears of corn still attached. Peel back the husks to reveal the colorful kernels, and invite your guests to snap one off to take home.

Harvest braids: Purchase or make braided ropes and garlands of autumn crops, such as grain, onions, miniature ears of corn, and so on. Hang them in the kitchen, around your hearth, over the altar, or from the fences if it's not raining and you're gathering outside.

Amber: Whether in the form of amber gemstone jewelry or golden-colored glassware, this color echoes the ripening fields of grain, the beginnings of fall leaves, and the dying rays of the sun. Use amber-colored glasses, plates, vases, and other items to add a warm glow to your surroundings.

Fall flowers: One of my very favorite flowers is the "naked lady" bulb, or *Amaryllis beladonna.* The highly fragrant, three-foot naked stems of large, rose-pink flowers appear only in very late summer through mid-fall, so Lughnassadh is a good time to gather some up if you can find them growing wild where an old homestead used to be. Sometimes you can find them at a florist shop or they can be special ordered. Another fall flower is the chrysanthemum, available in many sizes and colors. Load up the front porch with bright yellow spider mums and brighten the house with white and gold button mums.

Images of Lugh, Ceres/Demeter, Astarte, Corn Mother, other grain and harvest deities

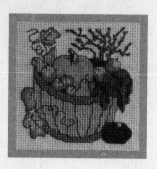

7

MABON/HARVEST HOME/FALL EQUINOX

(September 20–23)

There is a moment, one that's easy to miss if you're not used to noticing such things, that autumn arrives. It's a smell, really . . . a certain thickness to the air or ineffable fragrance that heralds its arrival. You won't be expecting it, but suddenly you sense that shift and know that the wheel has turned a little more . . . winter will soon be on the way.

Here in the western states, fall brings a paradoxical change in the form of rain. Just at the time when the year begins to show signs of death, the waters bring new life. Shoots of baby plants spring up as the deciduous trees become bare, and the hills turn green while the leaves turn brown. An interesting lesson, indeed.

There's also an odd sense of urgency when the first rains begin to fall, whether it's the need to harvest dry grains before they mildew or just to grab some forgotten items in the yard so they're not ruined. But it seems to be more than that—there's an electricity in the air (and I don't mean lightning, although that begins to appear too). Perhaps we're just sensing the atmospheric changes that come with a storm, and perhaps not. Maybe it's something more.

It's also the time when "nesting" begins, when comfy long-sleeved shirts are pressed into service, when the linens are changed from summer whites to flannel plaids, and when fireplaces are cleaned out in preparation of the ritual of coziness. The stores begin to carry harvest-theme decorations like preserved fall leaves, chrysanthemums, and pumpkins (and the really annoying stores begin to carry Christmas decorations). Activities turn toward the hearth and home as the yard is snugged in for the year, whether that means planting wildflower seeds, cleaning out the gutters, giving the lawn one last mowing, or beginning the task of splitting all that firewood.

Firewood keeps you warm three times it's said—first it's cut, then it's split, then it's burned. A home without a fireplace is like a cat without fur, and few things make me happier in the autumn than curling up next to the fire with a catalog or some embroidery. Of course, I'm a bit of a pyromaniac and I spend half the time playing with the darn thing, but that's part of what I love about fireplaces. I guess I'm especially fortunate because we live in an area that allows open burns on certain days, so my family and I often spend the entire day cutting out the overgrown brush on our mountain acreage and having huge bonfires. It's great fun and keeps us busy and warm on cold evenings.

Fall is the time of year that I also get the itch to start baking. It's cool enough during the day that running the oven won't make me sorry come bedtime, and it makes up for all the breads and cookies I wanted to make during the summer but couldn't. I always make at least one loaf of bread on Lughnassadh, no matter what the weather, but my real baking season starts around Mabon. Besides breads and sweet treats, I also love to make veggie-filled pot pies, casseroles, and other baked "comfort foods." It all goes back to the timeless urge to nest in autumn, the need for handmade crafts, soft blankets and sweaters, golds and muted colors, traditions both ancient and new, and the comforts of friends and family.

I honor Laxshmi as one of my primary deities. Although she is the Hindu goddess of wealth and fortune, most take this to mean material goods, especially money. But the lotus flowers in Laxshmi's hands indicate spiritual wealth and remind us that material wealth is not everything. Her lesson is that wealth appears in many forms besides cold hard cash, such as having a wonderful family, good health, an abundant vegetable garden, or richness in your spiritual life. Mabon is the time to recognize and be thankful for the abundance in our lives, whatever form that may take.

Acorn Processing

Years ago when I was a teen, I hung out with the Indians in Yosemite National Park a bit. (Note: Most native Californians prefer the term "Indian" to "Native American," so please don't write me indignant letters.) They were unfailingly kind and taught me many things, one of which was how to make acorns edible with traditional methods. There's actually a great book available on how to do this by one of the women who taught me, Julia Parker (see Appendix).

There's more to making acorn than just making it, however. It's an attitude, a way of being. It's also traditionally a woman's job only, so men, attempt this at your own risk.

Acorns were the primary staple food for the Indians of California, with other foods like meats, berries, other nuts, and roots coming after the nutritious acorn. So understand that without a good acorn crop, the People could starve in the winter. There are many traditional rules and tricks to working with acorn, the first of the season being "never look at green acorns in the tree." Julia would sometimes accidentally see them outside her office window and say to them, "You saw me, I didn't see you!" This would ensure that the acorns didn't feel their privacy was broken and provide a good harvest.

Acorns are tricky but generous, and people must be patient in all things. So ignore "first fall" of the acorns when all the wormy and diseased acorns fall from the tree about a month before the real crop comes ripe. When you first start seeing brown acorns falling, examine them and you will see tiny pinholes where the worms have been and the misshapen and moldy nuts. Sweep these out of the way so you don't pick them up by accident later on. The ones with their caps still on are no good either, so remove these as well. In a month or so, you'll be rewarded with a nice crop of fat, shiny, brown acorns.

These acorns are still unripe, so they need to be dried in the sun for a few days. If it's rainy weather during gathering season, try drying them on cookie sheets in your oven with just the light bulb or pilot light on. Dried and properly stored acorns can keep for several years, and they are traditionally one year old before being used, but "young" acorns like these are fine to use too. After a few days, they are ready to be shelled, winnowed, and then ground into flour. Ground into flour? Yep, you can't eat these things whole—the only way to effectively remove the bitter and toxic tannic acid is to grind the acorns into flour and wash the acid out of them (a process called leaching).

To pop the shells off the dry acorns, use a good hammer stone or an actual hammer. Set the nuts on end and give 'em a couple of firm taps. It will take some practice to get it just right—too soft and you won't split the shells, too hard and you'll pulverize the meats. After the nuts are out of the shells, check to see how dry the papery inner skins are. If they flake off easily, you're ready to proceed with the next step, but if they stick and are hard to get off, let the nutmeats dry in the sun (or the oven) for a few more days.

When the acorns tell you they're ready, carefully rub off the papery inner skin to leave only the clean, white meats. You may need to use a knife to split the nutmeats if they have folds that trap part of the skins (the acorns of some species, such as the black oak that's favored here in California, have these folds; others are smooth). In the old days, the elders used to give the younger girls the tedious job of skinning the acorns, with teasing being administered to any girl who left a bit of skin on her share.

If any of the acorns have *small* black spots inside, you can cut away the spotted part; otherwise, discard any black, rotten, or wormy nuts.

Winnow the nutmeats by placing several handfuls into a large, wide, flat basket. Don't use anything else, like a ceramic bowl or metal pan—you could bruise the nuts or lose some when they bounce off the hard surface. Fabric works okay, but you need two people and it's much more difficult to use than a basket. On a day with a slight breeze, go outside and toss the acorns into the air so that the papery skins blow away. Catch the nutmeats in your basket (this takes a little practice—don't try to toss them too high at first) and keep winnowing until all the skins are gone. If any bits of skin still cling to the nuts, rub them against each other and against the basket, then winnow again.

Once the acorn is cleaned, it will need to be ground into very fine flour. Traditionally this was done in granite mortars with heavy stones pounding the nutmeats into powder. Today's cook with an electric kitchen can grind the acorns into flour with a good blender or food processor and a fine sifter or wire mesh strainer. Place a handful of finished acorns into the blender and carefully grind them on the lowest setting or pulse power until they appear like fine flour. Do not grind them any longer than necessary or you'll end up with acorn butter (not a good thing, since the bitter tannic acid isn't out of the nuts yet). Take the flour out of the blender and sift it so that any larger bits of acorn are removed. Put these bits back in the blender and add more nuts. Continue until all the nuts are made into an even, fine flour. Any large bits of nut that find their way into the flour will not leach properly and will be a bitter surprise later on.

To leach the acorn flour, you'll need a large handkerchief, small pillowcase, small flour sack, or you can make a small sack by stitching linen dishcloths into a bag with one open end. Pour in the finely ground flour and fill the sack with water. When all the water has run out, tie the sack closed and then tie it to a faucet. Let the faucet run a little bit on the sack all night long to leach out the bitter tannic acid. In the morning, untie the sack and taste a little of the flour—if it's bitter, let it leach longer. If the flour is sweet, pour it out on a cookie sheet and allow it to dry, stirring it if necessary to ensure even drying.

The flour is now ready to be made into soup, cookies, bread, ice cream, or anything else. Store any unused flour in the freezer in a tightly sealed plastic bag to eliminate any stray odors or flavors. Acorn flour is an excellent natural thickener, so besides using it for flavor alone, use it in soups, cooked puddings, sauces, stir fry, and other thickened dishes.

Walnut Hulling

If you have walnut trees, especially the native American black walnuts, you and your guests can make hulling the nuts part of the Mabon festivities. The hull (also called a husk) is the green papery outer covering of the nut's shell. English walnuts, the ones we usually see used in baking and candies, don't usually need a lot of attention, and as the photo shows, the hulls usually dry up and come away from the shells easily. Black walnuts, shaken from the tree when the green hulls become soft and the nuts begin to fall, must have their moist hulls removed before the nuts absorb their bitter flavor or decay springs up in the hulls.

One way to remove the hulls from black walnuts is to let them dry in the sun on a gravel area for a few days and then drive over them with your car—this will loosen the hulls but not harm the extremely tough shells. Another method that may work when you have guests is to lay the walnuts outside on the ground, and have people walk, jump, and dance over them during the course of the ritual—just make sure you're doing this on bare earth or gravel and people have sensible shoes on to avoid turned ankles or sore insteps.

Other methods I've seen people use to remove the hulls are to force the nuts through a hole that's just big enough to let the shells through but strips off the green covering and rolling the nuts under a board or even balancing on the board like a circus act. When handling the hulls, always wear gloves so you don't stain your hands.

When you have finally removed them, save those hulls! Black walnut hulls are a popular herbal remedy used in the treatment of internal parasites as they are high in iodine, chromium, and other minerals. Hulls also make a fine dark brown natural dye without mordant, although you can use an iron pot if you want it to last a bit longer in your fabric and wish a nearly black color (remember to use gloves so you don't dye your hands!). The shells of the black walnut are also quite decorative, so after you've picked the meats out, paint them to make owl faces, sand the round backs off to make buttons and beads, or find ways of your own to use the hard shells artistically.

Cracking open English walnuts is easy, but you'll need a hammer for black walnut shells. Set them up on end and hit them right on the seam to pop them in half, then pick the meats out or continue to break apart the shells. This can take some practice to avoid smashing the nut-meats inside. The reward is a unique and delicious treat indeed.

Crop Harvesting Party

As a gardener, there's really nothing I like better than harvesting my flowers and vegetables. Watching the plants grow, the flowers bloom, the fruits of my labors and of the Earth ripen . . . all culminate in that final joyful moment when they're plucked and placed in the basket, still warm from the sun or wet from the rain. Part of that fun for me is selecting the varieties that my family loves to eat, or in the case of flowers, the most interesting and floriferous species and varieties for the cutting garden.

As part of my temple work, I keep a cutting garden and bring fresh flowers to our monthly meeting for the central altar. I also use them on my personal altar and around the house. They are grown with love, respect, and perhaps a pinch of magic. Naturally my vegetables do more than just feed my family—they are honored as gifts from the Green Man and the Earth Mother.

If you don't have a garden of some sort, plant one! Even if you're in an apartment, you can grow a surprising amount on a balcony or sunny windowsill. If you do have a vegetable garden or, better yet, heavily laden fruit trees, make sure to include their harvest in your Mabon ritual and festivities. Give everyone a basket or other container and tell them how best to harvest whatever crop you've focused on before starting. Or, if your garden is smaller, designate one person per crop and be sure each one knows what he or she is doing so you don't end up with damaged produce—you don't want shovel cuts in the potatoes and squished blackberries.

Sing songs as you work, and be sure to take it easy and have fun. When the harvesting is finished, take a large basket inside and place some of the harvest on the altar in thanks, while placing the rest aside for your guests to enjoy. If you have more than you know what to do with (zucchini anyone?), have extra paper sacks or baskets on hand so guests can take some of the bounty home. Aside from just making soup or pies, they will also be reminded of the day's Mabon ritual and can use the fresh produce in their own homes for a more direct connection to the Lord and Lady.

Putting Up With Autumn

This is your last chance to hold on to your summer produce crop as winter is on the way. Perhaps where you live you've already seen hard frosts by the equinox—in that case you'll need to think about preserving your fruits and veggies earlier than Mabon. Long before refrigeration, and even before one of Napoleon's men devised how to preserve peas in a glass wine bottle, our ancestors spent many fall days preparing fruits, vegetables, dairy products, and meats to be kept as long into the winter as possible, also called putting up, putting by, stocking up, and so on. Common methods were (and are) overwintering right in the garden, drying, using a root cellar, keeping produce and dairy products in cold water, salting, brine preservation (pickling), and sugaring. Modern preservers also have the luxury of freezing, canning (in both metal cans and glass jars), vacuum sealing, refrigeration, and so on.

Ideally, you should decide what kind of preserved products you want to have in the winter before you even pick out your seeds. Some kinds of tomatoes, for example, are great fresh on salads but turn to mush when you try to put them up in glass jars. Some plums are grown to be eaten ripe from the tree, and some varieties are specifically intended to be dried into prunes and have a higher sugar content. The list goes on and on, so check to be sure the varieties you select and grow will do what you want when it's time for the harvest.

If you can make a root cellar where you live, it's a great place to keep some fruits and vegetables into the winter without having to work with boiling liquids or take up all your freezer space. Ideally, a root cellar would have a vent near the floor on one side and another vent near the roof on the other to ensure good air flow and bring in cool air while venting warmer air. Many people use their basement as a root cellar in colder areas. Use empty boxes, grape crates, or half barrels and fill them with sawdust, then loosely pack in crops like hard shell squashes, root vegetables, unripe tomatoes, apples, and other good keepers. As with any kind of preservation, make sure your produce is unblemished to avoid premature rot and periodically check for spoilage so that one bad apple doesn't spoil the barrel (yep, that's where the expression came from).

Drying is another excellent way of preserving fruits, vegetables, and meats. If you expect a week or so of hot, dry weather, you can use old clean window screens (or make drying screens) and put thinly sliced fruits, tomatoes, and even marinated beef out in the sun to dry, covering them with a single layer of cheesecloth to keep pests away. A safer and more convenient method, especially if you don't have that much to dry, is to use a food dryer. These easy-to-use gadgets are available most places where kitchen appliances are sold. Another drying technique is to make fruit leather by puréeing fruits with sugar or honey (or nothing) and spreading it out thinly on some plastic wrap. Place the wrap on cookie sheets in your oven and leave it on warm or just the pilot light, until it's leathery and no longer sticky, and you'll end up with a dried fruit snack the kids can't keep their hands off of.

Perhaps one of the most popular methods of preserving produce is canning. Put simply, this consists of cooking fruits or vegetables, putting them in cans or jars, and either sealing them for storage or boiling the jars further for a time before storing them. There are hundreds if not thousands of recipes for canning various fruits and vegetables, and canning is a relatively easy and efficient way to preserve foods for up to several years, if they are stored in a cool, dark, dry place.

It's very satisfying to be able to open a cupboard or go into the basement and see shelves full of colorful preserves, whole tomato plants hung upside down so the fruits can ripen, buckets of moist sand filled with carrots, and shelves full of winter squash ready to sustain your family until Yule or even longer if the variety is a particularly good keeper. You can look at them and not only say to yourself "I grew that," but also "I can keep my family fed with the work of my own hands all winter long."

Of course, canning parties are great fun when you have a crowd over to help. One person can shell peas, another can chop fruit, one can wash canning jars, and someone else can be in charge of bringing the discards out to the compost pile. You can all trade off when the work becomes tedious so that you're not stuck snapping the stems off a thousand beans by yourself. Each person should receive a can or jar of what he or she worked on in thanks and to supply a bit of the summer garden in the winter kitchen.

Clipping Ceremony

A traditional activity in England is "clipping," in which the churches are blessed for another year. This usually occurs the Sunday closest to September 19 or thereabouts. The parishioners begin by joining in a procession, complete with band, that encircles the church. Afterward everyone encircles the building and as much of the yard as there are people to do it, all holding hands. The people all move inward, then outward again three times, still holding hands as they move to and fro. Blessings and prayers are said for the church, with all participating and holding their beloved church in their hearts. The church has now been "clipped," which is another term for "embraced."

A clipping ceremony would be a perfect ritual to perform with a large group of people, especially if you have a permanent circle or other ritual location. Have all participants hold hands while you tell the story of the ritual area. They could then dance deosil around the circle, holding hands or not, and say blessings for the land in the year to come.

Stone Circles

Circle Sanctuary has a tradition for their main ritual circle that I really like a lot—they encourage visitors to bring stones and add them to the ever-growing ring that surrounds the ritual area. This leaves a bit of the participants' energies with Circle, brings stones (and shells, crystals, medallions, gemstones, etc.) from all over the world to resonate on Circle land, and increases the size and power of the ritual area. Have your guests bring stones or other items to add to your ritual circle. If you don't have a stone circle set up like the one at Circle Sanctuary, you can bury the items at the four quarters of your space or start a circle now.

Perhaps the most perfect time to start a stone circle is on one of the equinoxes. Set your center stone in the exact middle of your ritual area and use a cord or other measure to make an exact circle around the stone (tie a screwdriver to the end of the cord and scribe a circle in the soil). Find out the exact time of the equinox in your area, and plan on getting up early that morning or the next day. At the sunrise closest to the exact time of the equinox, Set your eastern stone (or cairn of stones) so that its shadow falls on your center stone. At sunset, set the western stone in the same way. Measure out the halfway point between these stones and set your northern and southern stones in their proper places. Over the years, you can add more smaller stones to the outer edges of the ring and increase the size of the four quarter stones if you like, replacing them on the equinox and rededicating the sacred space each year.

Horn Dance

You may be familiar with morris dancing as a way of "waking up the Earth" in the spring, and I discuss this a bit in the Ostara chapter. However, an extremely old traditional morris dance is the Horn Dance, which is performed in the fall. It's so old, in fact, that the reindeer antlers used were collected in Britain before the animal became extinct there, which predates the Norman conquest. The dancers hold pairs of antlers in their hands and clack them together as they face off in two lines. Obviously, this is an imitation of the fights performed by wild deer as they determine who will lead the herd and who will have the best mate through the winter to come. The dance has been embraced by many Pagan groups who use it to symbolize the clash between the oak and holly kings, recognition of the Horned God, and the strength of the forces of nature.

The origin of the Horn Dance is uncertain, but it is best preserved as the Abbots Bromley Horn Dance which dates from at least 1226 and possibly 1065 or earlier. Early in the morning, the centuries-old reindeer antlers are gathered from inside the Church of St. Nicholas at Blithfield Parrish and the characters begin their almost twenty-mile, twelve-hour-long dance. Six of the dancers carry the horns, and there is also a Fool, Hobby Horse, Robin Hood, and Maid Marion who dance as well. As the group reaches a wayside house, farm, pub or other building, the group forms a circle that breaks into two lines where the horns are touched gently together or almost touched symbolically (due to their age they are much too fragile to "clack" together), then a circle again, then one line which takes them to the next building. It's a real test of stamina on the part of the dancers, but there's never any lack of people vying for a chance to be in the Horn Dance each year.

CRAFTS

Mabon Stitchery

The richness of the harvest flows from this bushel basket filled with all kinds of seasonal produce. Thirteen colors of floss, including a variegated brick red for the bittersweet berries, enliven this piece. (For additional stitchery instructions and suggestions, see pages 211–214.)

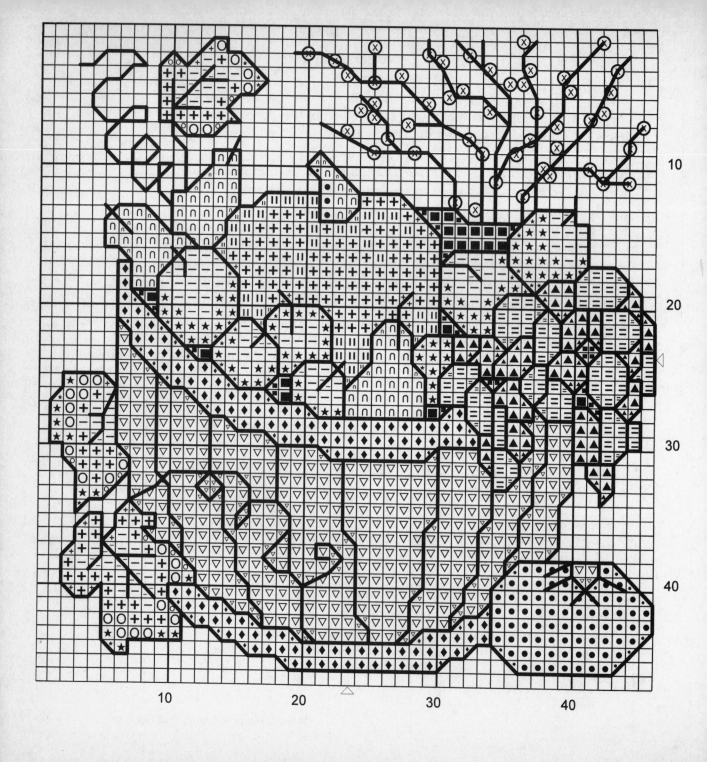

Grid Size: 47 W × 47 H
Cloth Count: 18
Fabric: Ivory Aida
Design Area: 2.61″ W × 2.61″ H (45 × 46 stitches)

Pattern Key

Symbol	DMC Floss		Color
■	898	(2 strands)	Coffee brown—very dark
△	902	(2 strands)	Garnet—very dark
=	3721	(2 strands)	Shell pink—dark
★	666	(2 strands)	Christmas red—bright
—	3822	(2 strands)	Straw—light
∩	3348	(2 strands)	Yellow green—light
▽	739	(2 strands)	Tan—very light
◆	437	(2 strands)	Tan—light
+	741	(2 strands)	Tangerine—medium
‖	721	(2 strands)	Orange spice—medium
•	890	(2 strands)	Pistachio green—very dark
O	946	(2 strands)	Burnt orange—medium
X	69	(2 strands)	Variegated brick red

Backstitches

Symbol	DMC Floss		Color
——	898	(1 strand)	Coffee brown—very dark

Note: The dots with X symbols are French knots. They call for the color indicated by the X symbol in the color key (DMC-69) and require two strands.

Corn Ladder

This traditional Southwest Indian craft is easy to make. Sometimes corn ladders were made very long for the practical task of drying ears of corn for winter, and sometimes they were made for ceremonial purposes with only four ears—one ear each of the four sacred colors of corn— blue, white, red and yellow. I made my example with some scraps of black denim left over from a sewing project for a rustic look.

YOU'LL NEED:

8 ears dried "Indian" corn
2 or 3 strips of sturdy cloth, approx. 1 inch by 40 inches
Raffia, dried flowers, silk flowers, etc. (optional)

Lay out the ears of corn on a table in a row, alternating the ends of the ears so that the pointy end of one ear is up against the fat stalk end of the next ear (see photo in the second insert). Arrange the corn so that it's pleasing to your eye—alternate light/dark/light, start with dark at the bottom and graduate to light at the top, mix the colors randomly, place the largest ear at the bottom and the smallest at the top, whatever you like.

Find the center point of each strip of cloth. Beginning at the bottom of your ladder, place the bottom ear of corn in the center of the cloth strips, each strip being about 2 inches in from each end of the ear. Firmly cross the strip over the top of the ear and lay the bottom halves of the strips on the table. Notice which way you have crossed the fabric and cross the strips the same way each time. Place the next ear on the strips and cross them over again. Repeat until all eight ears are securely woven into the strips of fabric. If you have enough fabric to make a hanger, tie a knot in each strip above the top ear of corn to secure it, then tie the ends of the strips together to make a hanger. Or add another strip at the top to make a hanger by simply tying it on to the top knot that secures the top ear of corn in place. Add raffia or other decorations to the knots if desired.

Corn Husk Dolls

Corn husk dolls are a very old craft, one which apparently originated with the Northeastern and Southeastern Native American tribes, such as the Iroquois, Oneida, Mohawk, Chickasaw, and Seneca. From the advent of corn as a food crop and enlargement of the grass teocinte into the large ears of modern maize, the craft of making things from corn husks grew. The faces of the dolls are usually left blank, and one legend tells of a vain and mean woman made from corn who was punished by the Great Spirit and made to wander the Earth forever faceless.

YOU'LL NEED:

Husks and dried silk from an ear of corn
Large bowl
Warm water
Scissors
Thin cotton string or embroidery floss
Craft glue

Soak the corn husks in the bowl full of warm water until they are very soft and pliable. Dampen the silk by dunking it under the warm water and gently running your fingers over it a few times. Select a couple of nice clean husks without blemishes and make a sandwich of them with the silk in the middle. Tie the ends of the husks and the silk tightly with the string about 1 inch down from the end. To make the head, fold the husks back on themselves to make a ball with the silk coming out of the center top of this ball. Tie the husks at the neck and arrange the damp silk to form hair, tying and gluing it as needed for the natural look of hair. The two husks will now form the outer body and dress of the doll.

To make the arms, roll a length of husk up to a diameter of about ¼ inch and tie it off at 1 inch and at about 4 inches from the first tie. Trim to ½ inch past the ties to form the arms and hands. Slip the arm roll up inside the husks until it touches where the neck is tied, centering it so the two arms are the same length. Trim two more husks flat on one end, roll them loosely together, and slip them up under the outer body/dress husks until they touch the arm roll. Tie the husks tightly about 1 inch under the arm roll to form the waist. Now simply trim the skirt as short as you'd like and when dry, the doll will stand up on this trimmed skirt edge.

Using a decorative woven braid for the waist tie makes a very nice accent. You can also dye the husks as desired, and add husk accessories like a contrasting apron. I have some old husk dolls I inherited from my grandfather that are a little angel band, with cornhusk wings, songbook, drum, and cymbals. You could make a cornhusk man by splitting the husks and tying off the ankles to make pants.

Gourd Container

Aside from the usual varnished, colorful, warty gourds you find at the grocery store this time of year, there are many varieties of smooth gourds used to make everything from earrings to bird houses, masks to lidded bowls. You can also just paint the whole gourd for a festive holiday decoration, and some varieties are bred and grown just for this purpose, such as the 'Penguin' or the 'Speckled Swan' gourds which really do look like birds with gracefully arching necks.

The gourds must be dried completely before using them in crafts and as containers. Experienced gourd artists like to line them up on a sunny windowsill or in another warm, dry location so that the gourds, which are really hard-shelled squashes, won't mildew or rot. When the gourd is fully dried, you can usually hear the seeds rattling around inside the shell, and when tapped it sounds like the shell of a rattle or maraca (which is traditionally a gourd). The gourd shell should be buffed with a nylon stocking or 0000 steel wool to clean and prepare the surface for painting.

YOU'LL NEED:

1 dried and cleaned gourd
Pencil
Drill
⅛-inch drill bit
Miniature keyhole saw
Metal spoon or gourd scraper tool
60-grit sandpaper
150-grit sandpaper
1-inch soft paintbrush

First determine if your gourd has a front and back (like a Yule tree—turn any unattractive blemishes to the back if it's symmetrical). To ensure an easy-to-fit lid on your container, make a notch or pattern in the seam where the lid meets the bowl that can only fit one way. Draw this on your gourd with a pencil—the design can be one notch, a zigzag pattern, a wavy line, a turtle with feet, or some other design to make it easy for you to put the lid back on.

In the back of the gourd using the line as a guide, drill a small hole through the gourd. It's best to make this hole on the inside corner of a zigzag or notch for the least visibility in the finished container. Place your miniature key saw in the hole and begin sawing the top off the gourd, following your pencil guideline. Take your time and work slowly to avoid chipping the gourd, especially if it has thin walls.

When you've got the gourd opened up, dump out any loose seeds (saving them to plant next year) and use the spoon or tool to scrape out as much of the dried innards as you can, paying special attention to ridges and bumps. Use the 60-grit sandpaper to remove most of the rough stuff inside, then move to the 150-grit paper for a final finish. Gently sand the edges of the box so that they're smooth but crisp. Use the paintbrush to clean off any remaining dust. Paint or decorate your gourd if desired and seal it, both inside and out, with nontoxic varnish if desired. These gourd containers make great gifts and fun projects for a gathering of friends, especially if you've precut the lids and all your friends have to do is decorate them.

Fall Leaf "Stained Glass"

I started making these when my son was a toddler. We would walk around our city neighborhood gathering colorful fall leaves, and when we got home he would arrange them on the paper and I'd iron them. I had so much fun that I'd sneak off to the kitchen and make more while he was asleep, then innocently claim to my husband that we'd both been creating them. The wax helps preserve their jewellike colors for months, so display the pictures in a sunny window where you can enjoy the stained-glass effect until Yule. Have your guests each go out and select a handful of leaves, then make them each a picture to take home. There's an example in the second photo insert.

YOU'LL NEED:

Iron
Old towel
Ironing board
Paper towels
A roll of wax paper
A selection of fall leaves in bright colors (thinner leaves like sweet gum, Chinese pistache, gingko, sugar maple, grape, etc., work best)
Scissors
Tape

Preheat your iron to "medium" or "wool" setting. Lay the towel on your ironing board or a flat table. Lay paper towels on top. Tear off two sheets of wax paper a little longer than you want your final picture to be and lay one on the paper towels. Arrange your leaves however you like to make a pretty picture. Carefully place the second sheet of wax paper on top, holding the bumpiest leaves down with your hand as you lay paper towels on top.

Gently iron the wax sheets together until no more air pockets can be eliminated around the leaves. Work on small areas at a time and carefully hold down each leaf as you iron, lifting the paper towel as you start on the next leaf to check its position. Don't press too long or too hot—you could scorch the leaves and ruin your picture. There will be some air pockets, especially around the stems of some leaves. Allow to cool and trim the edges of the paper. Attach to your window with a bit of tape and enjoy.

Fresh Fruit & Veggie Candleholders

These candleholders are easy to make and look incredible on the table. Make them the same day you plan to use them to avoid browning and shrinkage. Once you've got the candles lit and the holders in place, try arranging some nuts and fall leaves around the bottoms for additional color and texture (but make sure the leaves won't get near the flames if the candles burn down low).

YOU'LL NEED:

Several large apples, firm pears, miniature pumpkins, potatoes, etc.
Paring knife
Corer
Taper candles in coordinating colors, no taller than about 6 inches

Set the fruit or vegetable in question on the table and check to be sure it sits very straight and securely without any wobbling or tipping. This is very important for safety! Trim away some of the bottom with the knife if necessary to ensure that the holder will sit properly when finished. Use the corer to cut a circular hole halfway through the center of the fruit, twisting it to break off the partial core and create a cylindrical hole. If the center doesn't come out cleanly use the knife to cut out the core piece. Fit the taper inside the hole, enlarging the hole size if it won't go in or wrapping the bottom of the candle with a little plastic wrap if it's too loose. The candle should fit very snugly. Use immediately and surround with fall foliage, place in a bowl full of polished stones, or use as part of a floral centerpiece.

Silica-Preserved Flowers

Part of the altar-dressing for a recent ritual I did in honor of Bast was several vases full of red and white roses. One of my Temple brothers surprised me with two silica-preserved roses from the ritual and they are on my personal altar at this moment. I love the way the perfect form and color of the white and red roses have been so well preserved—they almost look alive. This technique works especially well with larger whole flowers that cannot be preserved easily or that are fleshy and prone to rotting with other drying methods.

YOU'LL NEED:

Fresh flowers, such as roses, gardenias, peonies, mums, etc.
About 1 cup of silica per small flower, or enough to cover
Dust mask
Shallow plastic container with a lid as tall as the flower to be dried
Small funnel or cream pitcher
Spoon

Cut the stem of the flower as short as possible. Spread about an inch of silica in the bottom of the container and stand the flower upright in it. Use a dust mask if necessary to avoid breathing the silica dust. Carefully surround the flower about halfway up with the silica, then begin pouring it between the petals gently. Pile more silica up around the flower and continue to sift silica between all the petals using the funnel, pitcher, or spoon, being careful not to distort the flower's shape and making sure each petal is surrounded with silica. When the flower is hidden completely and covered with at least 1/2 inch of silica, seal the container tightly and wait a few days. Open it up and check to see how dry the flower is—it should be papery but not brittle to the touch. The silica can be reused by drying it in an oven or microwave, and most brands have indicator crystals in the silica that turn a color if it contains moisture or if it's dry. Use the dried flowers in crafts or simply give them to your loved ones.

MENU

Sweet & Sour Walnuts

Individual Pot Pies

Willow's Harvest Bread

Autumn Fruit Crisp

Acorn Cookies

Apple Cider (Hot or Cold)

Sweet & Sour Walnuts

This delicious mélange features a number of interesting ingredients, but the star attraction is the walnut, which can be harvested any time in the fall through Samhain or even later if the weather is dry.

SAUCE

- ⅓ cup white vinegar
- ¼ cup pineapple juice
- 2 tablespoons soy sauce
- 2 tablespoons cornstarch
- ⅓ cup dark brown sugar
- 2 tablespoons honey
- 1 tablespoon fresh ginger, finely minced
- 1 clove garlic, finely minced
- 2 tablespoons vegetable oil
- 1 stalk celery, sliced thickly
- 1 carrot, sliced round or on an angle to make ovals
- 3 cups English walnut halves
- 2 cups fresh pineapple, cut into chunks
- 1½ cups tomatoes, cut into chunks
- 1 orange, peeled and cut into chunks

Steamed rice, preferably jasmine or basmati

To make the sauce, mix vinegar, pineapple juice, and soy sauce in a small saucepan. Stir in cornstarch until well blended. Add brown sugar, honey, ginger, and garlic. Stir and whisk over low heat until thickened. Heat the oil in a skillet or wok over medium-high heat, then add celery and carrot. Cook, stirring often, until tender but still crisp, then add walnuts, pineapple, tomatoes, and orange. Cook and stir until hot (do not overcook!) place on serving platter and pour sauce over to finish. Serve hot over steamed rice. 4–6 servings.

Individual Pot Pies

What do people want during the cold winter months? Comfort food! And what could be cozier than your own little pot pie, filled to capacity with delicious bite-size vegetables in a creamy sauce? Of course, eating the crust is half the fun (and flavor).

PIE CRUST

3	cups flour	1/3	cup butter
1	teaspoon salt	1	egg, beaten slightly
2	teaspoons fresh rosemary, minced fine	1	tablespoon white vinegar
1	cup shortening	5	tablespoons cold water

FILLING

2	tablespoons olive oil	1	carrot, cubed
1/2	yellow onion, diced	1	15-ounce can kidney beans
2	cloves garlic, minced fine	1	15-ounce can creamed corn
1/2	cup water	1	cup frozen or fresh peas

To make the crust, mix the flour, salt, and rosemary in a large bowl. Cut in the shortening and butter with a fork until the mixture is crumbly. Add the egg, vinegar, and water, mix until blended into a nice dough, but don't overstir or the crust will be tough. Divide the dough into about half, and roll out one half on a floured surface until about ⅛ inch thick. Cut to fit dishes. Roll out the other half of dough when needed, store any extra dough in the freezer for future use. Line four small (four-inch) or two large (six-inch) custard dishes with crust dough, make top crusts to fit over the dishes, set aside. Cut fanciful shapes in the top crusts with miniature cutters if desired.

To make the filling, heat the oil in a 2-quart pot over a medium-high heat and add the onion. Cook until soft, then add the garlic and cook for another minute or two. Add the water and carrots. Turn down to medium-low and cover, simmering the carrots until barely tender. Add the beans and liquid from the can, the corn, and the peas. Simmer over low heat about 15 minutes or until carrots are tender but not soft.

Fill the custard dishes until the mixture reaches just below the top and wet the edges of the crust dough. Lay on the top crust. Do not over-fill! Pinch the edges closed or use a fork to seal them tightly so no filling bubbles out the sides during baking. If no shapes were cut from the top crusts, make several slits in them with a sharp knife to allow any trapped steam to escape. Bake at 350 degrees for about 20 minutes or until the top crust is a nice golden brown. Serve hot. Makes 4 small or 2 large pot pies.

Willow's Harvest Bread

The trick to getting a nice high finished bread with this recipe is getting it from the mixing bowl and into the oven very quickly before the baking powder has time to fully react. And keep that oven door shut—no peeking!

About 3 cups pumpkin, kabocha, or other sweet winter squash, cubed	½ cup honey
	2 tablespoons vegetable oil
	1 cup cornmeal
2 eggs	¾ cup graham or whole-wheat flour
⅔ cup milk or buttermilk	2½ tablespoons baking powder

Preheat oven to 425 degrees F. and lightly grease a 9 × 9-inch baking pan. Steam squash until very soft, then mash into a pulp. Measure 1½ cups of pulp and pour into medium mixing bowl. Beat in egg, milk, honey, and oil until well blended. Add dry ingredients to squash mixture, stir until just blended, and quickly pour into pan. Place in oven immediately. Bake for about half an hour or until top begins to brown nicely. 6–9 servings.

Autumn Fruit Crisp

Savor the last of the year's fruits in this surprisingly rich dessert that has the added blessing of being very low in fat (of course, you can always serve it à la mode with vanilla ice cream). This dish is so easy it almost makes itself, and you can use any five combined cups of fruit you like best.

FILLING

1 cup fresh blackberries
1 cup soft ripe pears, cored and diced
1 cup tart red apples (like Fuji or Braeburn) peeled, cored, and diced or sliced thin
1 cup gooseberries (halved) or currants

½ cup pomegranate seeds
½ cup elderberries, stemmed and washed
¾ cup sugar
1 tablespoon flour

TOPPING

¾ cup rolled oats
½ cup dark brown sugar
¼ cup whole-wheat flour
½ teaspoon cinnamon
¼ teaspoon nutmeg

¼ teaspoon salt (optional)
¼ cup butter
½ cup chopped or minced pecans
¼ cup pine nuts (optional)

Mix fruits together in 9 × 9-inch square baking dish or large ceramic pie dish and sprinkle with sugar and flour, toss gently, and set aside. Mix together dry topping ingredients, then cut in butter until mixture is crumbly. Add nuts and sprinkle topping evenly over the fruit mixture. Bake at 375 degrees F. for about 30 minutes or until topping begins to brown and filling is bubbly. Serve hot. 6–8 servings.

Acorn Cookies

Some Elders don't like mixing acorn flour with nontraditional ingredients like wheat flour, feeling that it doesn't respect the acorn as a food worthy of standing alone. However, I feel this recipe highlights the beauty of acorn as a versatile and delicious food, and the other ingredients are the supporting cast to the star attraction. No disrespect is intended—to the contrary, I wish everyone would appreciate acorn as much as I do. Maybe this recipe will be a little stepping stone for people unfamiliar with its nutty and earthy qualities, and they can graduate to nuppa (traditional acorn soup) later.

½ cup butter	1 cup acorn flour
¼ cup shortening	1 cup whole-wheat flour
¾ cup granulated sugar	¼ cup wheat germ
1 egg	½ teaspoon salt
¼ cup milk	

Preheat oven to 375 degrees F. Cream butter, shortening, and sugar. Add egg and milk, beat until creamy. Mix in dry ingredients slowly until well blended. Drop by rounded spoonfuls onto lightly greased cookie sheet, press down slightly with sugared spoon or fingers. Bake about 10 minutes or until lightly browned all over. Makes about 2 dozen cookies.

DECORATIONS

Produce: Nothing displays the bounty of the fall harvest season better than fruits and vegetables. Populate your porch with pumpkins, make a creative display with flowering kale, cauliflower, colorful corn and other autumn veggies, make mountains of apples of all colors in baskets around the house, and garnish the table with colorful grapes still on the vine where a traditional centerpiece would be.

Nuts: These rich, brown, glossy seeds are beautiful and interesting structures that shouldn't be left out of your decorating efforts. Use small baskets full of nuts as table decorations, perhaps placing a name card between the nuts as part of your seating arrangements if you're having a formal dinner. Drill holes in acorns and string them like garlands, glue nuts to Styrofoam shapes and hang them as ornaments over the buffet, and be sure to leave out a large ceramic bowl full of mixed nuts in their shells with nutcrackers and picks on the coffeetable.

Fall leaves and branches: If you're lucky enough to live in an area that features annual fall color, bring some of that natural beauty inside to fill large ceramic pitchers and ample glass vases. Even in areas not known for this show, you can likely find some decorative branches in your neighborhood or even your own backyard. Look for scarlet rose hips, multicolored sweet gum branches ('Liquidamber' varieties), berry-filled ivy vines, interesting dried grasses, yellowing willow leaves, and ornamental elderberries, to name just a few.

Chrysanthemums: This is one of the most spectacular floral shows of autumn. This flower comes in hundreds of colors and shapes, and many varieties can be planted in your garden for yearly shows. Potted chrysanthemums, as opposed to the cut variety from the florist, last much longer, use less pesticides in their growing, can be planted out after they finish blooming, come in a wider variety of colors, and are often available in miniature sizes for smaller indoor displays.

Hydrangeas: Even though they are really done for the year, this classic flower is ready to be picked and dried for a sublime fall and winter show in your home. So popular with the Victorians, hydrangeas are available in colors from green through mauve, pink, and bright blue.

Dried flowers: There's a virtually unending selection of dried flowers for display and arranging, especially when you create them yourself. Some kinds are naturally suited because of their low moisture level and high visual impact when dried, such as the strawflower, love-in-a-mist pods, gomphrena, statice, and the paper daisy, all of which are commonly available at your local florist. Use them in bouquets or make swags, wreaths, garlands, place settings . . . your imagination is the only limit.

Images of Bacchus, Demeter/Ceres, other harvest deities

8

SAMHAIN/HALLOWEEN
(October 31–November 6)

In our "civilized" society, we are removed from a lot of things. Many children grow up having no concept of what meat is or where it comes from, many of us have online friends we have never met face to face, the truth about sexuality is hidden from our children while violence abounds in their television shows, and most of us have never touched or even seen a dead body.

Samhain is all about death. It's about the death of the year, the death of the crops and animals, the death of the Sun King and Lord of the Harvest, and if things don't go well in the winter, the possible death of us and our families. In many parts of the world, including on the streets of our cities, people die every year of the cold, so don't be lulled by a false sense of security that the old days of winter survival are gone. Many of us live from paycheck to paycheck, and many live without a paycheck at all. Tragedies happen. Wars happen. Life happens. Death happens.

The Funeral Ritual

I was twenty-four when my mom died suddenly, and I was devastated. My parents were divorced and my older sister was handling all the legal matters, so the funeral arrangements fell to me. It was hard, but it felt good to be in charge of it for some reason. I was able to take the time off work that I needed to go pick out a gravesite in the old pioneer cemetery, contact and meet a local minister who was a friend of my mother's, get some great John Muir quotes from the actor that performs his one-man shows in Yosemite Valley, and select and inscribe a head stone.

I dealt at length with the man that's both in charge of maintenance and who actually digs the graves. We sat under the huge oak tree and talked about what the service would be like as he checked my chosen site to be sure it wasn't already occupied (you never know in these pioneer cemeteries). He was most concerned with whether he would need to be present at the service, and I asked him to stand by since I honestly didn't know what I wanted. By the end of the service I'd actually forgotten all about him, but when I saw him shyly standing over to the side with his shovel, I knew the moment was right for him to come and gently sift the earth over the tiny box that held my mother's cremated remains.

I didn't realize it at the time, but that was my first public ritual. We invited the participants to help celebrate my mom's life, we stood in a circle and created an informal sacred space around the grave with love for her and each other, and as I placed her remains into the grave accompanied by an apt Muir quote, I definitely felt the energy peak and release in a flood of tears. The cemetery man was the wildcard, the ritual element that is unexpected but necessary in the end. The minister held it all together with her aplomb and strength, and although I planned the ritual and was the focal point of the energy, she was the true High Priestess. I virtually collapsed into her arms as the energy peaked and she held the framework together through experience.

Emotions run high at the close of the year, whether because we miss those that have passed over or because we sense the change in the air. The Sun King is dead, the crops have been taken by the frost, the days are growing colder and darker, and if you have one last chance to make sure you're ready for winter it's only through the weather's permission. Even in these modern times we can't help but gaze at the darkening skies and wonder if we really will make it to spring with nothing but a colorless world to look forward to.

But then we smile and know that spring will come, we can overwinter some of the crops, we've put enough into storage that we'll be fine. Perhaps we can take the opportunity to study this bleakness, to examine the structure of the tree that was hidden by the leaves, to enjoy the perfect whiteness of the snows and the passage of animals that we would have missed if their tracks were not left for us to find later. There is no better time to honor death and come to terms with it in our own personal way.

Remembering the Dead

After attending Starhawk's Spiral Dance in San Francisco one year, I decided to take part of that ritual home with me and now I keep a Litany of the Dead. Throughout the year I keep a list of those who have passed beyond the veil, those who have touched me in some way. On Samhain I recite the list of names, either in ritual with others or by myself, then I burn the paper and start again. It's one last tribute to their spirits as they make their way to the Summerland.

I also leave out a dumb supper offering on my altar to my ancestors, specifically my parents who have both passed over. I select their favorite foods and some extra goodies and leave the dishes out overnight as a gesture of love for them. I dress the altar when I can with marigolds, traditional in Mexico. The bright flowers are said to help guide the dead to their family's altar so that they may join in the festivities of Dias de los Muertos (Days of the Dead).

Samhain is also a time to laugh at death a bit. If we take it too seriously we become afraid of something that is inevitable for us all, so it's healthy to look at death with respect but also with a wink and a nod that says, "Yes, I know you're always there, but I'm not yours just yet." One of the focal points of my Samhain altar (see the photo in the second insert) is a small diorama from Mexico that depicts a rock band made up of skeletons. Such popular figurines are meant to be humorous, and I've seen everything from skeletal horse-drawn wedding carriages and bar pickup scenes to a skeletal Elvis.

Naturally, this sense of whimsy carries over to the usual Halloween activities of dressing up, trick-or-treating, and parties for kids of all ages. There are many theories of how dressing up and going door to door begging for treats started, but today it's an excuse to have fun, to be something you're not (or reveal something secret you really are), and to thumb your nose at death for a little while longer.

Of course, what would Samhain be without ghost stories? This one doesn't specifically involve a ghost, but it's one of my very favorite creepy and humorous "tails." I've rewritten it here with the storyteller in mind, and the parts can be read with any kind of accent you like, but I always think of it as either Irish, Scottish, or Cockney.

King o' the Cats

One cold evening at the beginning of winter, the gravedigger's wife was sitting by the fire, waiting for him to come home. Their old black cat Tom was sitting by the fire and seemed to be asleep, his eyes closed and a smile on his face. Suddenly, the gravedigger burst through the door, giving both his wife and the cat quite a fright.

"You'll never believe what I just saw!" he said breathlessly. "I was in the cemetery, a-diggin' old Mr. Fordyce's grave, when I must have dropped off for a moment. When what should awake me but the meowin' of cats!"

His wife and old Tom both stared at him. "Go on, go on," she said.

"Well, there I was, you see, a-sittin' next to the grave, when around the big oak tree comes this little black coffin, all draped in a little black pall, and what do you think was carryin' the whole affair?"

"What?" said his wife impatiently as she and old Tom both stared at him, their eyes growing bigger.

"Well, carryin' this little coffin was six or eight cats, all on their back legs a-walkin' along! And as they walked they all took a few steps and went 'Miow'. . . !"

"Miow!" said old Tom.

"Yes, just like that!" said the gravedigger. "So there I was, riveted to the spot, watchin' the procession, when the one in front turns and stares at me with these big yellow eyes . . . why, look at old Tom. He's starin' at me just like the other cat did!"

"Miow!" said old Tom, his eyes as big as saucers.

"So what happened next?" urged the gravedigger's wife.

"Oh, so as I was a-sayin', he turns and stares at me and then . . ."—the gravedigger started wringing his hands—". . . and then the cat turns to me and says, speaks to me I tell ye in a squeaky little voice, 'Tell Tom Tildrum that Tim Toldrum's dead.' Then he walks away! But who's Tom Tildrum?"

Suddenly the gravedigger's wife jumped up and shouted, "Look at Tom! Look at Tom!"

The old black cat was puffing up bigger and bigger, his fur all on end and his eyes glowing bright gold in the firelight. Then the cat said: "Wha-at? Tim Toldrum dead? Then I'm King o' the Cats!" And he rushed up the chimney and was never seen again.

Cemetery Cleanup

Besides telling creepy stories, there are many Samhain activities that are fun, ceremonial, or both. A cemetery cleanup is one project that is traditional to Mexican Day of the Dead activities and will make you feel great afterward. I usually visit my mother's grave and rake away the overgrown summer grasses, then plant bulbs or other flowers. If your relatives are in a cemetery that is strictly manicured and doesn't allow you to plant flowers, bring some grass clippers and trim any over-grown grass away from the headstone or other memorial plaque. If they're interred in a mausoleum or other building, bring some cleaning supplies and make it sparkle.

If you don't have any relatives buried nearby, you and your group can "adopt" a local cemetery and help clean it up on Samhain. Bring trash bags and pick up litter, bring gardening tools and clean up the gravesites, and bring flowers, flags, or other memorial items to set on the markers. Marigolds (either whole or sprinkled petals) and amaranth (loves-lies-bleeding, cockscomb) are beautiful and traditional Mexican choices for decorating graves. Of course, any flowers you wish to leave are greatly appreciated and show the dead that they are not forgotten.

Root Vegetable Lanterns

You might also choose to arrive at the cemetery in the evening with a lantern-lit procession. Before Halloween traditions were brought to America and pumpkins became the perfect vegetable for carving, tur-nips, mangles (a kind of giant beet), and large root vegetables called suedes were used for jack o'lanterns (and still are in parts of the British Isles). Suedes are closely related to sugarbeets, so choose the largest root of this type that you can find and hollow it out. Keep the top edges as thick as possible, and don't worry about making the bottom flat—you're making a hanging lantern. Carve whatever you like in the sides of the root, perhaps a face, some oak leaves, or an interesting pattern of holes. Make a contest out of it and have your guests vote for the best lantern. Punch two holes in each side of the top edge and tie some sturdy string on for a handle. Be sure to make it long enough that you don't burn your fingers! Add a votive candle and you're ready for your Samhain procession.

Stargazing

Another good outdoor activity for groups is stargazing. It might even be nice to spend the night in the cemetery in the Mexican style (assuming you're allowed to do this). They bring picnic meals to the gravesides of their loved ones, decorate the cemetery with festive tissue-paper garlands, flowers, candles, and so on, and have dinner with their beloved dead. After dinner, extinguish all the candles and leave one or two lanterns glowing. Bring a star chart to show the way and try to find as many constellations as you can. Play some appropriate music and enjoy the night sky—my favorite stargazing music is "Olias of Sunhillow" by Jon Anderson.

If you're not up for spending the evening that close to the dead or the weather prevents it, an indoor party may be more your style. Given here are several menus that you can build the theme of your party or gathering around: a silly party perfect for kids that features creepy foods; a more "adult" selection of seasonal and Samhain-themed dishes; and a potluck that features the favorite foods of your guests' beloved dead.

The Mystery Box

A game that's great fun, especially at a wilder party for kids, is the Mystery Box. Find a box that's roughly 24 inches on all sides or 24 inches square by 12 inches high. Seal up all the box flaps securely and cut four round holes about 4 or 5 inches in diameter in the sides, one hole to a side. Paint the entire box black and decorate it with skulls, ghosts, question marks, or whatever you like. Cover the holes with black felt and cut an **X** in the felt so that a person's hand will fit through the felt but the contents of the box will remain invisible. Find about twenty-five small, interesting objects to put inside the box, such as plastic toy animals, vampire teeth, fake skulls, etc. Make sure they have no sharp edges and that some items feel similar to other items.

On cardstock paper cut to about the size of playing cards, place a photo or drawing of each object and label the card. Place the stack on top of the box upside down and have your guests sit on all sides of the box. Turn over the first card, give people a few seconds to see what they're feeling for, and then turn them loose inside the box. Whoever finds the item pulls it out, shows the crowd, and keeps the card. If the wrong item has been chosen, the player must put it back and cannot search again until the next round. When all the cards and items are gone, the person with the most wins a prize.

Piñata Chaos

Another wild party game that works best outdoors is to break a piñata (you can get away with doing it indoors if you have a large open room free of breakables). Make a large skull piñata (instructions follow) and fill it with small wrapped candies that will pour out easily (sour-balls, butterscotch disks, Jolly Ranchers, caramels, etc.). String the piñata up from a tree branch or a hook in the ceiling and tie off the string loosely.

You can have your guests break the piñata a number of ways: You can give everyone a blindfold and stout stick and have them all go for it at once (somewhat dangerous!), you can give one person the blindfold and stick and spin her around several times before letting her try (a good method to use with kids), or you can do this and also move the piñata up and down by pulling on the rope (better for adults, it can be too frustrating for kids who keep missing). Once the piñata is broken, it's a free-for-all to grab as much candy as you can!

Nut-Crack Night

A more relaxed activity for an adult party is the tradition of popping chestnuts in the fire to foretell the future. Done on Samhain because it's an excellent night for divination, there are many ways to read what the chestnuts have to say—a loud pop may mean yes in answer to a question, a whistle could be a warning, a tiny pop or no pop at all could mean no, and if the chestnut jumps out of the pan that's a pretty dramatic answer to your question! Some people pop chestnuts on Yule instead of Samhain. Later, of course, you're welcome to eat the roasted chestnuts, but remember to leave a few out for the spirits to thank them for helping with the divination.

CRAFTS

Samhain Stitchery

The skies darken once again, and death reigns over all, as symbolized by this large skull design. The bone-colored image pops off the navy fabric, highlighted by the subtle sheen of rayon floss. (For additional stitchery instructions and suggestions, see pages 211–214.)

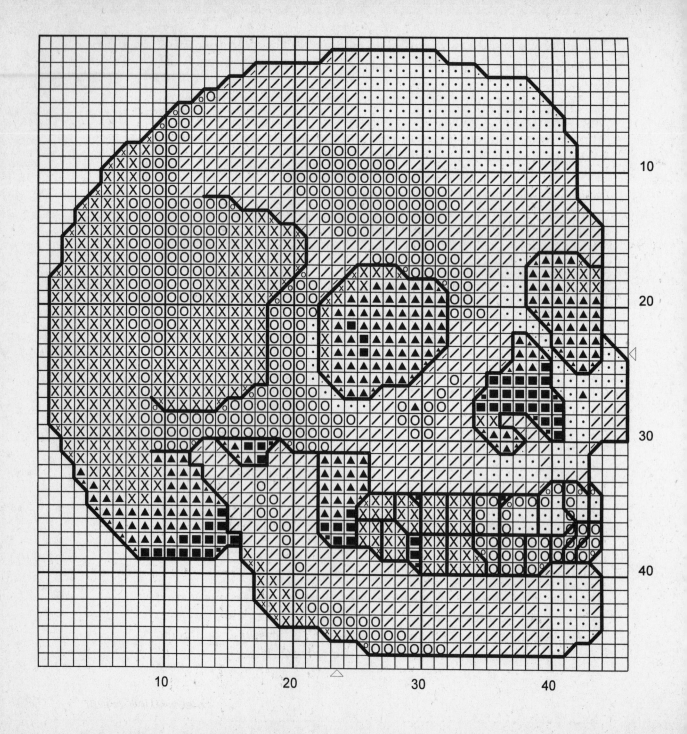

Grid Size: 47 W × 47 H
Cloth Count: 18
Fabric: Navy Aida
Design Area: 2.61″ W × 2.61″ H (45 × 46 stitches)

Pattern Key

Symbol	DMC Floss		Color
■	310	(2 strands)	Black
X	647	(2 strands)	Beaver gray—medium
/	712	(2 strands)	Cream
▲	535	(2 strands)	Ash gray—very light
o	3024	(2 strands)	Brown gray—very light
•	5200	(rayon, 1 strand)	Snow white

Backstitches

Symbol	DMC Floss		Color
——	310	(1 strand)	Black

Skull Piñata

This project is easy messy fun. Have a good time making and filling the piñata the day before, then hang it up at your get-together and give the skull a good smack so that the candy comes flying out for all to grab.

YOU'LL NEED:

1 extra-large pear-shaped party balloon
Newspapers
Large, shallow bowl or baking dish
White flour
Water
Craft or utility knife
2 or 3 yards of heavy cotton string
White acrylic craft paint or gesso
1-inch paintbrush
Black and white crepe papers
White glue
String for hanging the piñata

Blow up the large balloon to the size you want (at least 14 inches tall) and tie it closed. Tear the sections of newspaper in half horizontally, then tear these half pages into 1-inch strips down the length of the paper's grain (don't cut the papers—you want a ragged edge that will lay smoother when glued down).

In the large bowl, mix about ¹/₂ cup flour to 2 cups of water, adjusting the paste mixture so that it resembles thick cream in consistency. Dip the newspaper strips into the paste mixture and draw them gently between two fingers to remove any excess paste. Completely cover the balloon thickly with newspaper strips, leaving the knotted end of the balloon outside the paper. Allow to dry. Add a second thick coat of newspaper strips, laying them across the strips on the previous layer for added strength. Allow to dry.

Pop the balloon and remove it by pulling on the knotted end. If some balloon stays inside it doesn't really matter. Seal this hole with more newspaper strips (this is the bottom of the skull's jaw). Wrap the string around the shell several times so that it's secure, make a loop for hanging at the larger end of the shell and add more newspaper strips to help hold the string in place. Make sure the newspaper strips are not too wet and blot any excess paste off the shell—if it gets too wet without the balloon inside to hold its shape it could become dented or even collapse. Allow to dry completely.

Paint the entire shell white, allow to dry. Cut a 2-inch diameter hole near the top and fill the shell partially full with candy (don't overfill it to the brim or you may damage the shell). Tear irregularly shaped pieces out of white crepe paper and glue them thickly all over the shell to completely cover it and hide the candy hole. Out of the black crepe paper, cut two eyes, a nose, and either thin strips that can be assembled into grinning teeth or a "half moon" open smiling mouth. Glue the black shapes to the skull and it's ready to hang.

Sugar Skulls

There are two recipes for the sugar, two types of skulls to make, and two purposes for making them. Either make elaborate hollow skulls for ceremonial use only, or make small frosted skulls for eating (or make both!). The first sugar recipe is actually for making hollow panoramic Easter eggs, and the second is a more traditional Mexican sugar skull recipe. I included the first one in case you can't locate meringue powder (I also included an alternate Royal Icing recipe for the same reason).

YOU'LL NEED:

Large mixing bowl
Prepared sugar (see recipes below)
Plastic wrap or dampened kitchen towel
Sugar skull molds, any size
Pieces of cardboard to fit skulls

Spoon (if making large skulls)
Royal Icing (see recipe below)
Electric mixer
Medium mixing bowl
Several smaller bowls
Several zip-closure plastic freezer bags
Scissors
Colored foil, sequins, large beads, etc. (optional)

SUGAR RECIPE 1

4 cups granulated sugar
8 teaspoons water

SUGAR RECIPE 2

4 cups granulated sugar
4 teaspoons meringue powder
4 teaspoons water

ROYAL ICING 1

16 ounces powdered sugar, sifted
1/2 teaspoon cream of tartar
3 egg whites
Paste food coloring

ROYAL ICING 2

16 ounces powdered sugar, sifted
1/4 cup meringue powder
1/2 teaspoon cream of tartar
About 1/3 cup water
Paste food coloring

Do not attempt to make these on a humid day or if rain is in the forecast; the humidity in the air may cause the skulls to crumble. Dry weather is best, and if you're making them in advance for a crowd, the skulls will keep for weeks if stored in a cool, dry area. Also be sure your hands are absolutely clean as you work so you can eat the skulls if you wish.

In the large mixing bowl, combine the sugar and meringue powder (if using that recipe), blending thoroughly. Add the water by sprinkling it all over the sugar and mixing it by hand. The sugar mixture should form a "log" when squeezed in your hand—if it crumbles, add a few more drops of water until it's the right consistency. Keep the bowl covered when not in use to prevent the mixture from drying out as you work.

Press the sugar mixture very firmly into your skull molds, making sure to press sugar into every detail to avoid holes in the finished skull. Smooth and flatten the back of the skull with the cardboard, then flip the sugar skull out onto the cardboard and carefully set aside. They are quite fragile at this stage—allow them to dry undisturbed for 8 hours. The smaller skulls can be decorated at this point, but the large skulls are a two-part mold and the halves need to be hollowed out so they can be stuck together with Royal Icing. Cradle one half of the large skull in your hand and carefully scoop it out with a spoon, keeping at least $1/2$ inch in thickness. Repeat for the other half. The moist sugar that's scooped out can be used to make a couple of small skulls if desired (add a few drops of water if needed to achieve the right consistency). Allow these halves to dry completely overnight.

When you are ready to assemble and decorate the skulls, make the Royal Icing. In the medium bowl, combine the dry ingredients thoroughly. Add the liquid ingredient (eggs or water) and mix with an electric mixer on high for about 8 minutes or until quite stiff. Divide into smaller bowls and add the paste coloring (remember to keep one bowl white). As you finish each one, place each color in a zippered freezer bag and seal so the icing doesn't dry out, which it will do quickly if exposed to the air. To join the halves of the large skull, dust off the edges and snip a tiny corner off the freezer bag containing the white icing. Squeeze a thin rope of icing onto the edges and press the halves together firmly. Wipe off any excess icing and set aside to dry (about 2 hours).

When everything's dry, decorate your skulls. You can use traditional colored foils and other nonedible decorations for a beautiful altarpiece by "gluing" them on with Royal Icing. If you want to eat your skulls, simply use the assorted colors of Royal Icing and draw all over them to make teeth, eyes, abstract designs, or write the names of your ancestors and beloved dead on the forehead of your skull, a traditional Mexican practice. The skulls were also left on the graves of loved ones and personalized with foil eyeglasses, icing hair the appropriate color, and so on. An entire ritual, party, or quiet evening can center around making these colorful Samhain decorations and remembering those who have passed over. Makes 2 large or 8 medium or 40 small skulls.

Mugwort Dream Pillows

Samhain is an excellent time for divination because we are able to receive messages from the other side more easily and our natural psychic abilities are enhanced. This also makes it a perfect time for dreamwork, and these easy-to-make pillows contain an herb that helps you dream more vividly and prophetically.

YOU'LL NEED:

Scissors
Scraps of fabric at least 4$^{1/2}$ inches square
Matching thread
Sewing machine or sewing needles
12-inch stitchable hook-and-loop tape
    (without adhesive backing)
1 cup dried, chopped mugwort

Cut two fabric scraps so that they form a square about 4$^{1/2}$ inches across or a rectangle that's 4$^{1/2}$ × 6$^{1/2}$ inches. Place the fabric pieces right sides (printed or patterned sides) together and stitch them together along three sides, making your seam $^{1/4}$ inch in from the edge of the fabric. For the rectangle, stitch the two long sides and one short side.

Cut the hook-and-loop tape in half down the center of the strip so that it's about $^{3/8}$ inch wide. Hold the tape up to the open end of the pillow and cut a length of tape to match the opening (a little less than 4 inches). Separate the halves of tape. Fold the raw edges of the pillow over $^{3/8}$ inch. On each half, place one of the pieces of tape on the fold and stitch through all three layers a little less than $^{1/4}$ inch from the edge. Turn the pillow right side out and fill with mugwort. The hook-and-loop tape makes the pillow refillable, and, if you like, you can use other herbs, such as lavender, when not doing dreamwork.

Marigold Flower Pictures

Marigolds keep their color well when dried and making these pictures is a good way of using the flowers that were on your Samhain altar. Use the darker seeds as an interesting contrast to the pale yellow, golden orange, and paprika red of the flower petals. You can even plant the paper in spring and see what comes up.

> YOU'LL NEED:
> Construction paper, cardstock paper, Bristol board, or posterboard
>   cut to whatever size and shape you like
> White glue
> About 1–2 cups dried marigold flowers in assorted colors per picture

Begin with a sketched design on the posterboard if you like or design as you work. Spread glue thinly on an area of the picture and sprinkle or lay the marigold petals on to create whatever image you like, such as a bright yellow sun, an orange tiger, an impressionistic garden, or even a portrait of a loved one who has passed over. Allow the picture to dry, and place it on your altar so the spirits can find their way to it.

Shrunken Heads

Everyone will enjoy these wizened little heads, and they will be a big decorating hit with kids of all ages. Make them scary or happy, make them into Crones with a little wispy hair, or make them into Sages with long fuzzy beards. You can also start them at your gathering and let people take their creations home. (See insert.)

YOU'LL NEED:

1 ripe apple, any kind
Paring knife
Large mixing bowl (or bucket if you're making lots of heads)
3 cups water (or enough water to cover apples)
¼ cup salt
Black "pony" (3mm) glass beads
Acrylic craft paints
Wool doll hair or spinning fibers
Cloth doll bodies and clothing (optional)

Begin by peeling the apple and removing the stem. Cut away areas for the eyes, cutting a horizontal slit for each eye. Cut around the sides of the nose so that it protrudes from the cheeks. Cut a slit for the mouth and add any other details you like (round cheeks, cleft chin, ears, wrinkles, etc.). In a small bowl or large measuring cup combine the water and salt until the salt is dissolved and soak the apple in the salt water for about 10 minutes. Set the apple head where it won't be disturbed and allow it to dry so that it's leathery, about 2 weeks. You can also try drying it faster in a gas oven with just the pilot light on or the top of the fridge where it's warmer. Another drying method is to skewer the apple on a piece of wire (like a coathanger) and let the head hang from a cabinet knob for more even air circulation.

When the head is dry, slip glass beads into the eye slits for eyes, use diluted craft paints to add facial feature like lips and eyebrows, and add any hair or clothing you like with a bit of tacky craft glue.

MENU 1

Potluck with favorite foods of guests' beloved dead

Beverages

MENU 2

Pomegranate Salad

Black-and-White Chili

Pumpkin Yam Bake

Soul-a-Cake

Sugar Skulls

Sparkling Fruit Juices

Pomegranate Salad

Honor the dead with this delicious and colorful reminder of the sacrifice of Persephone and Demeter. Make sure the pomegranate is very dark red, shiny and fresh, not shriveled or unripe pink.

2   red apples, cored and cut into bite-size pieces

1   small jicama root, peeled and cubed

1   pear, cored and cut into bite-size pieces

1   blood orange, peeled, seeded and cut into bite-size pieces

The seeds of 1 large or 2 small pomegranates

Combine all ingredients except the blood orange and pomegranate seeds, tossing gently to mix them. Store covered in the refrigerator until ready to serve. Just before serving, add the blood orange pieces, toss, and sprinkle the pomegranate seeds on top. The blood orange is added at the last minute to avoid staining the white fruits. About 6 servings.

Black-and-White Chili

A wonderful color compliment to the Pomegranate Salad, this hearty chili is extremely low in fat and cholesterol and amazingly quick and easy to prepare. It looks especially festive when served with bright orange sharp Cheddar cheese.

2 tablespoons olive oil	1 tablespoon cornmeal
1 medium yellow onion, chopped	2 teaspoons chili powder
2 cloves (or 2 teaspoons) garlic, minced	1/2 teaspoon salt
	1/2 teaspoon cumin
1 15-ounce can black beans, drained	1 teaspoon unsweetened cocoa powder
1 15-ounce can white or navy beans, drained	1/4 teaspoon black pepper
1/4 cup water	Orange Cheddar cheese, grated
1/4 cup reserved bean liquid	Saltine crackers
2 tablespoons Classico Sun-Dried Tomato Sauce or minced sun-dried tomatoes	

Heat the oil in a 2-quart saucepan, add onions and sauté until translucent. While the onion is cooking, take about 1/3 cup of black beans and 1/3 cup of white beans and mix together in a bowl. Crush them with a fork and set aside. Add garlic and simmer another minute or until fragrant (do not overcook). Add both drained cans of beans and the crushed beans. Stir in the water, reserved bean liquid, tomatoes, spices, and cornmeal, mixing thoroughly. Simmer until thickened, about 5 minutes. Serve hot with cheese on top and crackers on the side. 4 servings.

Pumpkin Yam Bake

Nothing says autumn like sweet and golden pumpkins, which are an important part of modern Halloween festivities as well. Another fall vegetable that's similar in color and flavor is the "jewel" yam, and it makes a delicious addition to this spicy holiday casserole. This dish is extremely nutritious as well—it's an excellent source of potassium, vitamin A, vitamin B_6, fiber, ascorbic acid, beta carotene, and many other vitamins and minerals.

1 small (about 1 or 2 pounds) baking pumpkin, seeded, peeled, and cubed	1/2 cup golden raisins
	1/2 cup dark brown sugar
	1 teaspoon cinnamon
2 pounds red jewel yams, peeled and cubed	1/2 teaspoon ground ginger
	1/4 teaspoon ground allspice
1/2 cup dark raisins	

Combine the pumpkin and yam cubes in a steamer basket and steam for about 30 minutes or until quite soft. Transfer to a blender or food processor and blend until smooth, but don't whip. Pour this mixture into a large mixing bowl and add the remaining ingredients, blending thoroughly. Pour into a casserole dish and bake at 375 for about 25 minutes or until the edges begin to bubble. 8–10 servings.

Soul-a-Cake

This is the original treat part of "trick or treat." These delicious shortbread cookies were given as offerings to the dearly departed and the recipe is a re-creation of one that might have been used in medieval times.

3/4 cup butter, softened	1/4 teaspoon salt
3/4 cup light brown sugar	3/4 cup black walnuts
1 1/2 cups whole-wheat or graham flour	1/4 cup slivered almonds
1/2 teaspoon cinnamon	1/2 cup dried currants
1/4 teaspoon nutmeg	1/3 cup golden raisins

Cream together the butter and sugar with a fork, then add the remaining ingredients and blend well. Press into a lightly greased 9 × 9-inch square baking pan and prick several times with a fork. Bake at 350 degrees F. for about 20 minutes or until the edges just start to turn golden. Cut into bars or squares with a sharp knife while still warm and allow to cool before serving. Makes 16 medium or 20 small squares.

MENU 3

Rotting Skull Delight

Guts with Chunky "Blood" Sauce

Garlic Bone Bread

Gray Matter Gelatin

"Lady Fingers" (and Eyes) Cookies

Suspiciously Red Sparkling Citrus Punch

Rotting Skull Delight

This gruesome recipe is usually found on the Internet as "Meathead," and you are certainly welcome to make that fleshy variation if you prefer. Combine this recipe with the others below to make a whole corpse—on a long table first place the brain gelatin on the far left, then the skull, then lay out the bone bread for arms and legs (you can also make bread ribs), use the cookies for fingers and toes, and place the red guts in the middle of it all for maximum effect.

Plastic human skull
16 ounces fat-free cream cheese
3 large tomatoes, sliced thin
12 ounces jack or Swiss cheese slices
3 5.5-ounce packages Ives or other veggie lunchmeats (bologna, turkey, etc.)
1 12-ounce package precooked seitan, sliced thin
2 hard-boiled eggs
2 olive slices
Rolls and condiments for sandwiches

Wash and dry the human skull completely so that it's literally clean enough to eat off of, and place it on a large plate. Spread the cream cheese all over the skull, then begin layering tomato slices over the cream cheese, which will help them stick to the skull. Next add a layer of cheese slices over the tomatoes, starting at the top and overlapping them if you have trouble with the slices slipping off the sides. Cut the slices to fit smaller areas (bridge of the nose, around the teeth, etc.) as needed. Now add layers of lunchmeat slices over the cheese—you can get different effects with the different colors of luncheon meat so purchase turkey if you want a pasty zombie look, bologna for a fresh kill, salami for diseased meat, and so on. Cut the meats to fit as needed. Finally, add a layer of seitan over the lunchmeat for a nice rotting skin effect. Place the yolks from the hard-boiled eggs into the eye sockets and add olive slices for the pupils. Keep chilled until you're ready to serve with lettuce garnish and other sandwich fixings (remember to warn unsuspecting guests before they open your refrigerator).

Guts with Chunky "Blood" Sauce

Okay, it's just spaghetti with red sauce, but it looks great on the Samhain buffet table, especially when combined with Garlic Bone Bread. If it doesn't look scary enough for your tastes, toss in a couple of fake eyeballs and watch your guests squirm.

6 ounces uncooked spaghetti	1 tablespoon milk
1 tablespoon olive oil	2 teaspoons sugar
1 small onion, diced	1 teaspoon fresh rosemary, minced fine
1 tablespoon or 2 cloves garlic, minced	1/2 teaspoon fresh sage, minced fine
3 8-ounce cans tomato sauce	1/2 teaspoon salt
2 vine-ripened or 4 paste tomatoes, cut into chunks	1/4 teaspoon pepper
1/2 cup sun-dried tomatoes, plain or in oil	

In a large pot, boil about 8 cups of water and add the spaghetti, stirring occasionally and boiling until the pasta is cooked. Add a splash of cooking oil if desired to keep the pasta from sticking together. Turn off heat and allow to stand until ready to serve.

While the pasta is cooking, pour the oil into a 1 1/2 quart saucepan and heat over a medium flame. Add the onions, cooking until just transparent, then add the garlic and cook for another 30 seconds. Add the tomato sauce, then the remaining ingredients, and cook about 3 minutes or until the sauce begins to bubble. Lower the heat, cover, and simmer another 5 minutes, then turn off the heat and allow to stand another 5 minutes.

Drain the pasta completely and place back in the pot. Add the hot tomato sauce and stir gently to combine them completely. Serve in a large covered bowl with garlic bread and grated Italian hard cheeses (Parmesan, Asiago, Romano, etc.) on the side. 6–8 servings.

Garlic Bone Bread

This recipe combines the traditional Mexican *pan de los muertos* (bread of the dead) with enough yummy garlic that you won't be troubled by vampires for several days. It's the perfect compliment for the spaghetti recipe above.

1 tablespoon yeast	1 teaspoon salt
½ cup hot water	3 tablespoons (about 6–9 cloves)
1¼ cups milk	garlic, minced fine
About 5 cups flour	Garlic powder

In a small bowl, soften the yeast in the hot water. While the yeast is softening, heat the milk in a small saucepan to boiling, simmer for about 30 seconds, and remove from heat. In a large bowl, combine 4 cups of the flour with the salt and add the yeast mixture, scalded milk, and minced garlic. Stir the dough and add enough additional flour to form a dough that pulls away from the sides of the bowl and isn't too soft and sticky to handle. Knead on a well-floured surface about 8 minutes or until quite elastic. In a lightly oiled bowl, place the dough and cover it with a clean linen dishcloth. Allow to rise in a warm location for about an hour or until doubled (an excellent place for this is inside a gas oven with just the pilot light on or the top of your refrigerator). Punch down the dough, turn it out onto a floured surface, and divide the dough into 12 pieces. Form each piece into a little bone-shaped loaf and rub the top of each loaf with garlic powder. Place your bone loaves several inches apart on nonstick cookie sheets and allow to rise again, about 40 minutes. Bake at 375 degrees F. for about 15 minutes or until they begin to turn golden on the edges. Allow to cool 5 minutes and serve with butter and pasta. Makes 1 dozen mini-loaves.

Gray Matter Gelatin

If you're not concerned about making this recipe vegetarian, simply use 9 ounces of regular gelatin mix to fill the brain mold.

½ cup agar flakes
6 cups cherry cider (or your favorite fruit juice)

1 cup sugar
Green or black food coloring (optional)

This recipe should make enough to fill the more popular brain molds on the market, but you may want to measure the liquid capacity of the mold just to be sure and adjust the recipe as needed. Set up the mold in advance by rolling up a towel and making a circle with it on a cookie sheet, then setting the brain mold level in the towel. Spray the inside with a light coating of vegetable oil pan spray.

In a large saucepot, combine the agar flakes and 1 cup of the fruit juice. Over medium-high heat bring the mixture to a boil, then simmer for about 10 to 15 minutes or until the agar flakes have completely dissolved. Pour the remaining juice into a medium mixing bowl and add the agar mix and sugar, stirring until all the sugar has dissolved. Add a few drops of green liquid food coloring or a speck of black paste food coloring if desired to make the brain appear more realistically colored, whisking to blend completely. Pour the mixture into the mold and chill for several hours or until completely set. Chill until ready to serve, then wiggle the gelatin to loosen it from the mold and turn the brain out onto a serving plate garnished with lettuce or as desired. About 12 servings.

"Lady Fingers" (and Eyes) Cookies

I've made these delicious cookies for years. They can be molded into anything, not just body parts, but they do make fantastic creepy cookies for Samhain revelry. Because of their size, fingers and eyes are perhaps the most effective body parts to replicate in dough.

1 cup butter, softened	Food coloring
1/2 cup sugar	Clean small paintbrush
2 1/2 cups flour	Small container of clean water
1 teaspoon vanilla	1 tube red cake decorating gel
1/4 teaspoon ground allspice	(not frosting)
1 egg yolk, slightly beaten	

Combine the butter and sugar thoroughly. Add the flour, vanilla, and allspice, mixing to form a stiff dough. Decide what body parts you want to make, then divide the dough in portions for each body part. For example, if you're making fingers, eyes, hearts, and livers, divide the dough into four parts. Refrigerate for at least 30 minutes or longer (you can store the dough in the freezer for future use as well).

Use the food coloring to tint the dough to the desired color—leave eyeballs white. If you're making livers or some other darkly colored item, use paste food coloring so you don't dilute the dough. Knead the coloring into the dough carefully and use an apron. Form the cookies into the desired shapes and place on a nonstick or very lightly greased cookie sheet as you finish them. Each cookie should be about 1 inch in diameter and will spread slightly when baked. If the dough becomes too soft to work with, return it to the refrigerator until it stiffens sufficiently.

Divide the egg yolk into small containers and tint each a different color with the food coloring. Brush the colored egg yolk onto the cookies to form red fingernails, different eye colors, blue veins, and so on. Wash out the brush when changing colors. With the red decorating gel, create bloodshot eyes, arteries, and so on. The gel will stay shiny even after baking. Bake at 300 degrees F. for about 25 minutes or until the bottoms just begin to brown slightly. Do not overbake. Remove from cookie sheet carefully and cool completely. Makes about 2 1/2 dozen.

Suspiciously Red Sparkling Citrus Punch

A woman I used to know served a similar punch at all of her parties and boy, would it be gone fast! She soon learned to keep supplies for double and triple batches in the freezer to avoid guest revolts in the living room.

- 1 can frozen limeade concentrate
- 1 can frozen raspberry lemonade concentrate
- 1 can frozen Hawaiian Punch concentrate
- 2 liter bottle Cherry 7-Up, lemon-lime soda, or ginger ale

In a very large punch bowl, combine all ingredients, stirring gently to break up the frozen bits so that the carbonation won't be released and cause the punch to go flat. Serve with a ladle into punch cups. Serves 10–12.

DECORATIONS

Skulls and skeletons: Death! Death everywhere! And it looks really festive, too! Skulls and skeletons are my number-one Samhain decoration, and I've been able to find vintage skull mini-lights, tiny jointed skeleton mini-lights, skull wire garlands, a black door wreath with little skulls on it, and all kinds of jointed skeletons to hang from ceilings and porches. You can also find skeleton paper garlands at party stores, masks, plates and cups for the table, and more. I even got a set of plastic skeletal hand salad tongs a few years back! If you made one from this chapter, a skull piñata is the perfect thing to hang up and complete the theme.

Day of the Dead: They may be difficult to find except on the internet, but Dia de los Muertos items are fantastic things to add to your

Samhain party arsenal. Traditional Mexican Halloween celebrations focus on honoring loved ones who have passed on and laughing at death, so look for whimsical dioramas with skeletal people doing just about anything, sugar or clay skulls, colorful garlands made from cut tissue paper (*papel picados*), T-shirts, candles and candleholders, art prints, papier mâché items like jointed skeletons, fresh-cut marigolds, and other traditional Dia de los Muertos goods.

Ravens and vultures: These two black birds represent the same thing—death and the scavengers that come after. The raven is important in Celtic mythology, where it represents the Morrigan, the shape-shifting goddess of war and death. Vultures, besides their obvious connections to scavenging dead bodies, also represent several Egyptian deities, including the nature goddess Nekhbet or Nekhebet. If you have the good fortune to know a taxidermist or happen to find a stuffed raven or vulture at a flea market (you never know!), these would look great looming over the buffet table or over the back of the sofa in the shadows. Your guests could pose with them for photos, or you could hide them in the shadows of the bathroom to startle people. Use paper cutouts of ravens and vultures and hang them in the windows, make paper garlands, and wire small craft-store versions to houseplants and curtain rods.

Everything's gone black: Not just for funerals any more, black is a terrific Samhain party color. Make curtains of black crepe-paper streamers over all the doors or twist them up and hang them from the corners of the ceiling. Use black makeup, nail polish, wigs, and clothing for that Morticia Addams look. Hang black drapes or black lace over all the windows, even in the daytime, for a haunted-house effect. Decorate with garlands of black bats, put up a black "egg tree" made from a dried manzanita branch mounted on a base, much like the ones usually painted white for Easter. You can cover the tree with spiders and cobwebs, and if you've always wanted to paint your ceiling black, now's the perfect time to go for it.

Black light candles, bubbles, makeup, etc.: One of the absolute coolest and fun things to have at an evening Samhain gathering is glow-in-the-dark stuff. There are lots of items in stores at Halloween time that either glow by themselves or are activated by a black light. When buying a black light, make sure you get the largest one you can afford and that it's truly a UV black light, not just a regular light bulb painted dark purple. The bigger the light, the more brightly your reactive items will glow. You could set aside a "black light room" and go nuts with lights and glowing goodies in that one room for maximum effect on a small budget. Besides any regular glow-in-the-dark items and many white fabric items, other black light reactive things that can be purchased include makeup, novelty wigs and costumes, paints, bubbles, candles, and tons of Halloween items.

Images of Hecate, Kali, Anpu (Anubis), Ausar (Osiris)

APPENDIX—EMBROIDERY INSTRUCTIONS

Counted cross stitch is one of the easiest embroidery techniques, and a perfect starting place for beginners. You simply make lots of little X's in different colors to form your design on special fabric. All the designs in this book are done on 18-count (18 stitches to the inch) aida cloth, which is specially designed for cross stitch. If you're familiar with the technique you can certainly use any needlework fabric you like for the designs, such as other sizes of aida, pure linen, evenweave, and so on.

The charted designs are easy to follow, and I carefully selected the symbols for each color chart to make reading them as simple as possible. Each color of floss is represented by a black-and-white symbol in a grid, and each grid square is equal to one X stitch or square of aida cloth. It's almost like paint-by-numbers.

The floss is DMC cotton embroidery floss, available virtually everywhere needlework or sewing supplies are sold—it's one of the most popular brands in America. The metallic fibers are all from Kreinik, a brand available in specialty needlework stores, some large craft stores, and on the Internet. I like to use a number 5 embroidery needle, but other stitchers prefer a more blunt tip or a shorter needle, so you might want to get a variety pack of needles and experiment to find out what you like best. The last things you'll need are a small embroidery hoop (plastic, wood, or metal—any type you personally prefer) and a pair of embroidery scissors.

Before working with your fabric and fibers, wash and dry your hands to remove any traces of dirt, oils, hand lotion, and so on, which can discolor your work. Find a comfortable chair with good lighting for your embroidery to prevent fatigue. Cut a piece of aida cloth about 6 inches square and center it in the embroidery hoop, which should be about 4 inches in diameter. Pull the fabric taut in the hoop. Have all your supplies close at hand, perhaps in a sewing basket, so you can find what you need without having to get up to retrieve that skein of floss or pair of scissors from the other room.

Begin stitching at or near the center of your design because it allows the fabric to shift around a little without distorting the stitchery and it's easier to find your place. Because you're working on 18-count aida cloth, you'll only need two strands of floss to fill in the squares. Clip off an 18-inch length of floss, tease apart the strands at one end (there will be six) and slowly pull one strand out of the end while holding the others together gently. Don't be concerned by the apparent tangle of threads you're left with—simply set aside the single strand and pull the other end of the floss bundle gently downwards to gain a nice smooth length of floss again.

Take the single strand you pulled out and fold it exactly in half. Wet the ends slightly and thread them through the needle. To secure the floss for your first stitch, push the needle up through the corner of one little aida cloth square, down through the opposite corner, and through the loop in the end of the floss strand on the backside of your work. Pull snugly against the fabric to secure it. I usually go from upper right to lower left, then upper left to lower right to make my X, but you can do it the other direction if you prefer (be sure to make all your stitches go the same direction!). Some stitchers prefer to make all their initial diagonals one direction, then return to make all their second diagonal stitches, but I find this doesn't turn out as even. However, you should feel free to stitch however you like in order to get the best results.

To thread the metallics in the needle, pinch the end of the strand inside your fingertips firmly and push the ends carefully through your embroidery needle as you slowly open up your fingertips. If this technique doesn't work for you, try threading a folded piece of paper halfway through the eye of the needle, inserting the end of the fiber between the paper, and pushing both through the eye. The blending filaments are simply added to the regular cotton floss and threaded with them—use one strand of blending filament for two strands of floss, leave an extra long tail on the back to begin, and fold it up under the work you're currently doing so that the filament is well anchored under the back of each new stitch. The rayon is treated exactly like cotton floss.

Working from the center out, fill in areas of color. Half-stitches consist of a tiny single stitch made from one of the corner holes right into the center of the square (or from the center to a corner hole if it makes your work look neater). Fill in all whole and half stitches, then do all backstitching last of all.

Backstitching will smooth the edge of one half-stitch or divide two half-stitches. Backstitching is one single strand of floss unless otherwise instructed. To secure the beginning end of this strand, slip your needle under about 3/8 inch of stitchery on the back side of your work. Backtrack a few threads, then go another 1/4 inch or so to lock the thread in place. Pull the backstitching thread gently for the first couple of stitches to ensure that it doesn't pull out of the backside. End all stitching neatly on the backside by running under your previous stitching about 1/2 inch, then clip off the excess floss.

To finish your needlework, either gently iron it if not washable, or hand wash it gently in the sink with a tiny bit of quilt soap (available at quilting or craft shops), then block your work by pressing it with a warm iron (not hot!) on the back side while still damp. If using synthetic fibers, iron a test scrap first before proceeding so you don't accidentally melt all your hard work.

To make the Wheel of the Year wallhanging, use pins or dressmaker's pencil to mark a square 4 inches across that's centered on your design, following the grain of the aida cloth exactly. Stitch the nine squares together as shown, stitching exactly on the grain. Stitch the three squares of the top row together, then the middle row, then the bottom row, press the seams open, then stitch the three strips together into a square. Press the seams open and use fusible interfacing on the back of the piece. Mount, mat, and frame the piece as desired.

If you need to store your needlework, lay it flat inside acid-free tissue paper—folding needlework will leave creases that can be difficult to iron out later. If you store your needlework inside a plastic bag, be sure to leave the end open so that any moisture can escape, since trapped moisture inside a sealed plastic bag can spell a nasty death by mildew to needlework (this goes for any fabric or paper items stored in plastic).

Grid Size: 47 W × 47 H
Cloth Count: 18
Fabric: Gray Aida
Design Area: 2.61″ W × 2.61″ H (45 × 45 stitches)

Pattern Key

Symbol	DMC Floss		Color
■	310	(2 strands)	Black
+	433 + 435	(1 strand each)	Brown—medium & brown—very light
•	White	(2 strands)	White

Backstitches

Symbol	DMC Floss		Color
——	310	(2 strands for letters and star border, 1 strand for wheel border)	Black

RESOURCES

YULE

Flint-and-steel fire starting supplies

Hollowtop Outdoor Primitive School, P.O. Box 697, Pony, MT 59747-0697, (406) 685-3222, www.hollowtop.com

Ragweed Forge, P.O. Box 326, Sanborn, NY 14132, www.ragweedforge.com

Sparks Fly Striker Co., 10 River Rd. RR#3, Hackettstown, NJ 07840, (908)852-6834, www.scoutskills.com/products.htm

Hand shadows

Fun With Hand Shadows, by Sati Achath and Bala Chandran. New York: McGraw-Hill, 1996.

Hand Shadows and More Hand Shadows, by Henry Bursill. New York: Dover Publications, 1997.

Shadow puppets

Worlds of Shadow: Teaching with Shadow Puppetry, by David and Donna Wisniewski. Greenwood Village, Col.: Teacher Ideas Press, 1997.

Wassailing chants

The Stations of the Sun: A History of the Ritual Year in Britain, by Ronald Hutton. London: Oxford University Press, 1996.

Nontoxic varnish

J. W. Etc., 2205 First St., Suite 103, Simi Valley, CA 93065, (805) 526-5066, www.jwetc.com

IMBOLC

Handspinning supplies

Acorn Street Shop, 2818 N.E. 55th St., Seattle, WA 98105, (800) 987-6354, www.acornstreet.com

Dragonfly Farms, Studio Gaustad, 11178 Upper Previtali Rd., Jackson CA 95642, (209) 223-3602, http://pweb.jps.net/~gaustad/index.html

Halcyon Yarn, 12 School St., Bath, ME 04530, (800) 341-0282, www.halcyonyarn.com

The Joy of Handspinning, 128 College Dr., Edison, NJ 08817, (888) 345-5460, www.joyofhandspinning.com

Candle-making supplies

Alberta Beeswax and Candle Supplies, 10611-170 St., Edmonton, Alberta, Canada T5P 4W2, (780) 413-0350, www.candlesandbeeswax.com

The Barker Company, 15106 10th Ave. S.W., Seattle, WA 98166, (800) 543-0601, www.barkerco.com

Hearthsong, 1950 Waldorf NW, Grand Rapids, MI 49550-7100, (800) 325-2502, www.hearthsong.com

Yaley Enterprises, 7664 Avianca Dr., Redding, CA 96002, (877) 365-5212, www.yaley.com

Battery-powered Santa Lucia crowns

Marcus International, P.O. Box 8042, St. Paul, MN 55108-8042, (612) 645-8578, http://members.aol.com/SwedMarcus/SwedMarcus/

Skandinavian Link, 1707 West Kirby Ave., Champaign, IL 61821, (866) 356-4646, www.skandinavianlink.com

Sonika's Too, 5922 Portage Rd., DeForest, WI 53532, (877) 766-4527, www.sonikas.com

Canapé and mini cookie cutters

Fairy Gardens, P.O. Box 5351, Lynnwood, WA 98046-5351, (425) 774-0936, www.fairygardens.com

Kitchen Krafts, P.O. Box 442, Waukon, IA 52172, (800) 776-0575, www.kitchenkrafts.com

Sweet Celebrations, 7009 Washington Ave. South, Edina, MN 55439, (800) 328-6722, www.sweetc.com

OSTARA

Raising chickens

ABC of Poultry Raising: A Complete Guide for the Beginner or Expert, by J. H. Florea. New York: Dover Publications, 1977.

Chickens in Your Backyard: A Beginner's Guide, by Rick and Gail
  Luttmann. Emmaus, Pa.: Rodale Press, 1976.
Raising Poultry Successfully, by Will Graves. Charlotte, Vt.: Williamson
  Publishing, 1985.
Storey's Guide to Raising Chickens, by Gail Damerow. Pownal, Vt.:
  Storey Books, 2001.

BELTANE

Birds and Birdhouses

Attracting Birds, by Phyllis Elving. Menlo Park, Cal.: Sunset Publishing
  Co., 2000.
*Attracting Birds to Your Backyard : 536 Ways to Turn Your Yard and
  Garden into a Haven for Your Favorite Birds*, by Sally Roth. Emmaus,
  Pa.: Rodale Press, 1998.
Wild Birds Unlimited, 11711 N. College Ave., Suite 146, Carmel, IN
  46032, (317) 571-7100, www.wbu.com

Fiddlehead ferns, fresh

Earthy Delights, 1161 E. Clark Rd., Suite 260, DeWitt, MI 48820, (800)
  367-4709 or (517) 668-2402, www.earthy.com
The Maine Lobster Shop, (877) 474-4763 or (207) 498-8181,
  www.mainelobstershop.com

Fiddlehead ferns, canned

Maine Goodies, PO Box 288, Albion, ME 04910, (866) 385-6238 or (207)
  437-2052, www.mainegoodies.com
The Maine Lobster Shop (see above)

LITHA

Gold-panning supplies

D & K Detector Sales Inc., 13809 SE Division St., Portland, OR 97236,
  (800) 542-4653, www.dk-nugget.com
K.J. Traders, P.O. Box 54, Forbestown, CA 95941, (530) 675-9202,
  http://kjtraders.com/

Heliograph (sun print) supplies

Fabrics to Dye For, Two River Rd., Pawcatuck, CT 06379, (888)
  322.1319, www.fabricstodyefor.com/Pebeo
Nature Print Paper, P.O. Box 314, Moraga, CA 94556, www.natureprint
  paper.com

LUGHNASSADH

Grains for backyard growers

Abundant Life Seed Foundation, P.O. Box 772, Port Townsend, WA 98368, (360) 385-5660, www.abundantlifeseed.org

Baker Creek Heirloom Seed Co., 2278 Baker Creek Rd., Mansfield, MO 65704, (417) 924-8917, www.rareseeds.com

Territorial Seed Company, P.O. Box 158, Cottage Grove, OR 97424, (541) 942-9547, www.territorialseed.com

Southern Exposure Seed Exchange, P.O. Box 460, Mineral, VA 23117, (540) 894-9480, www.southernexposure.com

Corn-shucking and grain-harvesting equipment

Cumberland General Store, #1 Highway 68, Crossville, TN 38555, (800) 334-4640, www.cumberlandgeneral.com

Lehman's Hardware and Appliances, Inc., P.O. Box 41, Kidron, OH 44636, (330) 857-1111, www.lehmans.com

Southern Exposure Seed Exchange (see above)

Wheat weaving supplies

Campus Granary, Bethel College Women's Assn., North Newton, KS 67117, (316) 283-3940, www.bethelks.edu/womenassoc/

Country Straw Pickin's, Box 44, Frontier, Saskatchewan, Canada S0N 0W0, (306) 296-4952, www.commercemarketplace.com/shops/countrystraw/

Jack's Grain and Gourds, 14105 Rowley Rd., Durand, IL 61024-9689, (815) 248-4073, www.homestead.com/jacksgrainandgourds/index.html

Sylvan Flower Farm, Box 1025, RR, Sylvan Lake, Alberta, Canada T4S1X6, (877) 700-2808, http://bdcg.com/slflower/

MABON

Acorn preparation

It Will Live Forever, by Beverly Ortiz and Julia Parker. Berkeley, Cal.: Heyday Books, 1996.

Food preservation supplies

Ball Blue Book: Guide to Home Canning, Freezing and Dehydration. Rye, N.Y.: Alltrista Corp., 1997.

Stocking Up: The Third Edition of the Classic Preserving Guide, by Carol Hupping. Emmaus, Pa.: Rodale Press, 1990.

Cumberland General Store, #1 Highway 68, Crossville, TN 38555, (800) 334-4640, www.cumberlandgeneral.com

Kitchen Krafts, P.O. Box 442, Waukon, IA 52172, (800) 776-0575, www.kitchenkrafts.com

Lehman's Hardware and Appliances, Inc., P.O. Box 41, Kidron, OH 44636, (330) 857-1111, www.lehmans.com

Gourd craft supplies

Gourds by Jeanie, 6305 W. Argent St., Pasco, WA 99301, (509) 545-4443, www.gourdsbyjeanie.com

Ozark Country Creations, 30226 Holly Rd., Pierce City, MO 65723, (417) 476-5454, www.ozarkcountrycreations.com

Pumpkin Hollow, 610 CR 336, Piggott, AR 72454, (870) 598-3568, www.pumpkinhollow.com

Sandlady's Gourd Farm, RR4 Box 86, Tangier, IN 47952, (765) 498-5428, www.sandlady.com

SAMHAIN

Brain gelatin mold

Archie McPhee & Company, P.O. Box 30852, Seattle, WA 98103, (425) 349-3009, www.mcphee.com

Anatomical Chart Company, 8221 N. Kimball, Skokie, IL 60076, (800) 621-7500 ext. 235, www.boneyardbargains.com

Autopsy Services, (800) 288-6779, www.1800autopsy.com (slightly more expensive, but a portion of the proceeds goes to charity)

Sugar skull molds and supplies

CRIZMAC Inc., P.O. Box 65928, Tucson, AZ 85728, (800) 913-8555, www.crizmac.com/sugarskulls.html

Reign Trading Company, 3838 Walnut Grove Blvd., Rosemead, CA 91770, (626) 307-7755, www.mexicansugarskulls.com

Black lights and UV novelties

Blacklight Volleyball, 50 Needle Blvd. #30, Merritt Island, FL 32953, (877) 677-4537, www.blacklightvolleyball.com (Complete UV catalog, not just volleyballs.)

Proformance Entertainment and Theatrical Products, P.O. Box 3177, Beverly, MA 01915, (978) 922-3277, www.proformance.net/index1.htm

INDEX

ABOUT THE AUTHOR

WILLOW POLSON is a born and raised Californian, and has been a Witch since the age of thirteen. Wandering in and out of many paths, she categorizes herself as "Eclectic Wiccan" when pressed, although her main ritual outlet is an Egyptian ritual group currently based on her land near Yosemite National Park. Willow plans to erect a temple there and to create a castle and medieval-themed retreat center as well.

Willow is one of the co-creators of *Veggie Life* magazine, one of the largest vegetarian cooking magazines in the world, and has been on the staff of other internationally popular magazines, including *Needlepoint Plus*, *Tole World*, and *Popular Woodworking*. She has been in publishing for over twelve years and is also the author of *Witch Crafts: 101 Projects for Creative Pagans*. She is currently a member of several national needlecraft and Pagan rights organizations and has won awards for her embroidery and artwork.

When not writing or doing needlework, Willow enjoys gardening, working on her mountain property, instigating live action role playing (LARP) adventures, playing with her five cats, watching improv comedy, and dreaming about castles. For further info, tips, news, craft ideas, recipes and more, visit www.willowsplace.com.